The Gospel of John

THE "STUDY HOUR" SERIES . . .

The Acts of the Apostles
The Gospel of John
The Gospel of Mark

Study Hour
Commentaries

The Gospel of John

Introduction and Notes by
W. GRAHAM SCROGGIE
D.D. (Edin.)

LONDON
PICKERING & INGLIS LTD.

PICKERING & INGLIS LTD

ISBN 0 7208 0381 0
Cat. No. 01/0713

THE GOSPEL OF JOHN

All rights reserved. No portion of this book may be reproduced in any form without the written permission of the publishers.

Reprinted by special arrangement with Pickering & Inglis, Ltd.

First Zondervan printing   1976

Library of Congress Cataloging in Publication Data
Bible. N.T. John. English.   1976.
  The Gospel of John.
  Reprint of the ed. published by Marshall, Morgan & Scott, London, under title: St. John; issued in the Study hour series.
  1. Bible. N.T. John — Commentaries.
I. Scroggie, William Graham, 1877-1958.   II.   Title.
III.   Series: The Study hour series.
BS2613 1976   226'.5'077   75-42049

Printed in the United States of America

INTRODUCTION

Key-note: " BEHOLD THY GOD."

Written in Ephesus. Written for the Church.

Eagle-like Aspect. The Gospel of Wisdom.

Date 90–100, A.D.

The writer of this Book was John, the son of Zebedee and Salome, "the disciple whom Jesus loved," and who leaned upon His breast at the Last Supper. There can be little doubt that he wrote toward the close of the first century, and was at the time the last surviving of the Apostles. More than twenty years before, the Holy City and Temple had been destroyed by the Romans, and the Jews finally scattered. But previous to that, the entire New Testament had been written, with the exception of John's contributions, so that, no doubt, he was instructed in the teaching of his brother Apostles, and had special facilities for writing concerning the Lord in the light of subsequent developments.

John was the living link that united the two great ages of past and future, for he commenced his ministry at a time when Judaism was most expectant, and ended it at a time when Christianity had thoroughly rooted itself in the world.

It need hardly be remarked that this Record is entirely different from the previous three; "Conversations, miracles, contacts with others, intercourse with the disciples—all are different"; but contrasts are not necessarily contradictions. There were whole cycles of events, relations, and experiences, which the Synoptists had not touched: vast spaces of truth which they had left unfilled, but which, in due time, were filled by one who, by temperament and circumstance, was specially qualified to render this unique service.

About a generation after the ascension of Jesus, grave error had arisen concerning His Person; error which Paul combats in his Epistle to the Colossians; and this most probably had become wide-spread by the end of the first century. It seems quite clear that John had such heresies in mind when he wrote, for three of his five Writings are an unfolding of the Person of the Lord Jesus Christ. The " Gospel " is designed to show that Jesus was the Divine Son; the first Epistle presents the Divine Son as Jesus; and the Apocalypse, as the name signifies, is a final unfolding of the power and glory of Jesus Christ, the Divine Son.

It may be said that the Gospels are the heart of the Bible, and that John's Record is the heart of the Gospels; it is the Holy of Holies in the Temple of Truth. Almost everything here is new. John alone gives us a glimpse into the first year of our Lord's ministry (ii.–iv.); he alone records the great discourses on the New Birth, the Living Water, the Bread of Life, the Good Shepherd, the Light of the World, together with that marvellous unfolding of His purposes to the disciples at the Last Supper (xiii.–xvi.). Eight miracles only are recorded by John, six of which are peculiar to his Gospel.

But it is not only what is said that gives distinction to this narrative; what is not said is equally significant. There are here no genealogy, no birth, no boyhood or growth, no baptism, no temptation, and no Gethsemane: everything is directed to the end in view, to prove that Jesus was God. " These things are written that ye might believe that Jesus is the Christ, the Son of God, and that believing ye might have life through His name " (xx. 31). The whole book is a witness to this truth, and " witness " is one of the keywords of the Book. It occurs about fifty times in these pages, and calls attention to the word of the Baptist, of the Evangelist, of Philip, of Nathanael, of Nicodemus, of the Samaritan Woman, of the Nobleman, of Martha, of the Scriptures, of the Works, of Christ Himself, and of the Father in attestation of Jesus' Divinity. The growing unbelief reflected in chapters v.–xii, xviii.–xix. is unbelief in the claim of Jesus to be Divine: and the growing belief reflected in chapters xiii.–xvii., xx., is belief in Christ as the Son of God. The entire Book gathers around this truth, and men are blessed or unblessed according to their attitude to this self-revelation of Christ.

But this is not all. A careful examination of the Prologue to this Gospel (i. 1–18) will furnish us with a simple, but complete analysis of its spiritual content.

Here, the Son is revealed, first, as the Eternal Life, " in beginning," with God, and very God, and the Creator of all life, from the Seraphim to the worm (1–5). Then He is revealed as the Eternal Light, the Light of men which shines in the darkness, of which John came to bear witness, and which was not comprehended (6–13). And finally, He is revealed as the Eternal Love, made flesh, and dwelling among men, full of grace and truth, and imparting to men of His fulness (14–18).

This threefold revelation enters into the substance of the entire Book, and is the key to its structure. Speaking broadly, it is Christ as Life Who is manifested to the World in i. 19—xii.; Christ as Light Who is presented to the Disciples in xiii.–xvii.; and Christ as Love Who is revealed to all, on the Cross, through the Tomb, and in Resurrection, in xviii.–xxi.

But this distributive analysis is by no means exclusive; in each of these divisions we may trace the Life, the Light, and the Love.

For instance in the first section (see Analysis) the Life Announced (i. 19–ii. 11); the witness of the Baptist is concerning Life (19–34), that of the Disciples, concerning Light (35–51), and that of the Feast, concerning Love (ii. 1–11).

In the second section, the Life Acknowledged (ii. 12—iv. 54), the same order is observable. Christ is Life to Nicodemus (iii.); **Light to the Samaritan**

Woman (iv.); and Love to the Nobleman (iv.). In the third section (v.–xii.) it is first the Life that is despised (v.–vi.), then the Light that is refused (vii.–ix.) and finally the Love that is outraged (x.).

Nor is this remarkable fact less evident in the second main division of the Book (xiii.–xvii.), but the order is inverted. In dealing with the World the thought moved from Life to Love; from the fount of blessing to the overflow; but in dealing with the Disciples, it moves from Love to Life, from the overflow of blessing to the fount. The Love is manifested in the opening proceedings of the Last Supper (xiii. 1–30) the Light in the discourse which followed (xiii. 31—xvi.) and the Life in the Intercessory Prayer, which places Christ in anticipation beyond death and the grave, and in Glory with His Father.

In the third division (xviii.–xxi.), which tells of the Sufferings of Christ, it was Life that was laid down, it was Light that was put out, and it was Love that was nailed to the Cross: but Life emerges from the grave (xx. 1–18), Light breaks in dazzling brilliance on the wondering disciples (xx. 19–31), and Love gives its final earthly tokens to the loved (xxi.).

It is impossible for us to over-estimate the importance of this profound revelation, for it is the very hub of truth. The Divine Nature, Work, Method, Fellowship, Mercy, and Grace, are all gathered up in this, that the Son is Life, and Light, and Love, and every blessing, both present, and prospective must be within the compass of this truth, and must flow out from it, as every sin is a wrong done, on the part of man, to Christ in one or other or all of these aspects. The truth may be summarised as follows:—

There are here,

I. THREE ASPECTS OF THE DIVINE NATURE.

    (i.) Life, the Energy of God.
    (ii.) Light, the Intelligence of God.
    (iii.) Love, the Character of God.

II. **THREE PHASES OF THE DIVINE WORK.**
   - (i.) Regeneration by the Life.
   - (ii.) Illumination through the Light.
   - (iii.) Assimilation to the Love.

III. **THREE LINES OF THE DIVINE METHOD.**
   - (i.) Life by the Cross.
   - (ii.) Light by the Word.
   - (iii.) Love by the Spirit.

IV. **THREE PLANES OF DIVINE FELLOWSHIP.**
   - (i.) Having Life, bearing " fruit." (xv. 2).
   - (ii.) Having Light, bearing " more fruit." (xv. 2).
   - (iii.) Having Love, bearing " much fruit." (xv. 5).

V. **THREE APPEALS IN DIVINE MERCY.**
   - (i.) The Life appeals to our Will.
   - (ii.) The Light appeals to our Mind.
   - (iii.) The Love appeals to our Heart.

VI. **THREE SINS AGAINST DIVINE GRACE.**
   - (i.) To Resist the Spirit is to refuse the Life. (Acts vii. 52).
   - (ii.) To Quench the Spirit is to despise the Light. (1 Thess. v. 19).
   - (iii.) To Grieve the Spirit is to wound the Love. (Eph. iv. 30).

Trace in this Gospel the development, side by side, of faith and unbelief. Look up all the references to " life," and discover whether natural life (*Bios*), or spiritual life (*Zoe*), is meant. Make a list of words peculiar to John, such as " Overcome," " Verily, Verily," " Paraclete." Follow out the development of teaching concerning the Spirit, in this Book, possibly the last written of the inspired Scriptures. Find out how often Christ speaks of having been " sent " by, and from God, and how often He declares that His message is that which He received of the Father.

Trace also the following words, each of which occurs twenty times, or more: Glory, Glorify, To gaze upon, Light, Truth, World, Witness, Know, Works, Name, and Father. Trace also the forty-two Old Testament quotations or allusions in this Gospel. Also, there are not less than fourteen conversations of Jesus with men and women, which should be carefully studied; as should be also the sevenfold witness to Christ in this Record.

Wonderful indeed is this Gospel. No praise of it can be exaggerated. "It is the unique, tender, genuine, leading Gospel" (*Luther*). "The most important portion of the New Testament" (*Lessing*). "It is a voice of thunder, and yet more love-bewitching and elevating in its influence than all the harmonies of music" (*Chrysostom*). It is "the heart of Christ" (*Ernesti*). "It possesses a peculiar originality and charm to which there is no parallel" (*Tholock*). It is "the diamond amongst the Gospels, which reflects the glory of the Godhead, even in the crown of thorns" (*Lange*). "It is the Gospel of the world, resolving reason into tuition, and faith into insight" (*Westcott*). "It is the noiseless completion of the inner and holier places of the temple of faith" (*Alford*). It is "a river deep enough for an elephant to swim, with shallows where a lamb may wade" (*Owen*).

OUTLINE OF THE GOSPEL

PROLOGUE: *THE PAST* i. 1–18.
    (a) The Divine Life Revealed, 1–5.
    (b) The Divine Light Displayed, 6–13.
    (c) The Divine Love Expressed, 14–18.

PART A
THE REVELATION OF GOD AS LIFE TO THE WORLD i. 19–xii. 50.

I. THE LIFE ANNOUNCED, i. 19–ii. 22.
  1. The Witness of the Baptist, i. 19–34.
  2. The Witness of the First Disciples, i. 35–51.
  3. The Witness of the Works, ii. 1–22.

II. THE LIFE ACKNOWLEDGED, ii. 23–iv. 54.
  1. In Judea, South, ii. 23–iii. 36.
  2. In Samaria, Centre, iv. 1–42.
  3. In Galilee, North, iv. 43–54.

III. THE LIFE ANTAGONISED, v–xii.
  1. *The Controversy Aroused*, v. 1–47.
    (i.) Love Displayed, v. 1–18.
    (ii.) Light Revealed, v. 19–47.
    (iii.) Life Presented, v. 39, 40.
  2. *The Controversy Developed*, vi.–x.
    (i.) The Life Despised, vi.
    (ii.) The Light Refused, vii.–ix.
    (iii.) The Love Outraged, x.
  3. *The Controversy Concluded*, xi.–xii.
    (i.) The Love Sympathising, xi. 1–37.
    (ii.) The Life Saving, xi. 38–xii. 11.
    (iii.) The Light Shining, xii. 12–50.

PART B
THE REVELATION OF GOD AS LIGHT TO THE DISCIPLES xiii–xvii

I. INTRODUCTION TO THE LIGHT FOR THEM, xiii. 1–30.
  1. The Light expressing Love, 1–20.
  2. The Light exposing Hate, 21–30.

II. IMPARTATION OF THE LIGHT TO THEM, xiii. 31–xvi. 33.
  1. *In the House*, xiii. 31–xiv. 31.
     (i.) Separation and Reunion, xiii. 31–xiv. 4.
     (ii.) The Way to the Father, xiv. 5–11.
     (iii.) The Coming of the Comforter, xiv. 12–27.
     (iv.) The Gain of Loss, xiv. 28–31.
  2. *On the Way*, xv.–xvi.
     (i.) Vital and Fruitful Union, xv. 1–16.
     (ii.) The Enmity of the World, xv. 17–xvi. 6.
     (iii.) The Work of the Spirit, xvi. 7–15.
     (iv.) The Encouraging Farewell, xvi. 16–33.
III. INTERCESSION FOR THE LIGHT IN THEM, xvii.
  1. Christ and the Father, 1–5.
  2. Christ and the Disciples, 6–19.
  3. Christ and the Church, 20–26.

PART C
THE REVELATION OF GOD AS LOVE TO ALL xviii.-xx.

I. THE TRIAL OF DIVINE LOVE, xviii. 1–xix. 16.
  1. Betrayal and Arrest, xviii. 1–11.
  2. Jewish and Roman Examination, xviii. 12–xix. 16.
II. THE TRAGEDY OF DIVINE LOVE, xix. 17–42.
  1. The Crucifixion, xix. 17–30.
  2. The Burial, xix. 31–42.
III. THE TRIUMPH OF DIVINE LOVE, xx.
  1. The Great Discovery, 1–10.
  2. Love Rewarded, 11–18.
  3. Peace for Fear, 19–23.
  4. Certainty for Doubt, 24–29.
  5. The Purpose of the Record, 30, 31.
EPILOGUE: *THE FUTURE*, xxi.
  (*a*) The Life Attracting, 1–14.
  (*b*) The Love Appealing, 15–17.
  (*c*) The Light Assuring, 18–25.

This Gospel may be viewed from numerous standpoints, and the scheme will vary with each, so that any outline can be suggestive only.

ST. JOHN 1. 1-18

Title: IMMANUEL : GOD WITH US

1 In the beginning was the Word, and the Word was with God, and the Word was God. 2 The same was in the beginning with God. 3 All things were made by him ; and without him was not any thing made that was made. 4 In him was life ; and the life was the light of men. 5 And the light shineth in darkness ; and the darkness comprehended it not.

6 There was a man sent from God, whose name was John. 7 The same came for a witness, to bear witness of the Light, that all men through him might believe. 8 He was not that Light, but was sent to bear witness of that Light. 9 That was the true Light, which lighteth every man that cometh into the world. 10 He was in the world, and the world was made by him, and the world knew him not. 11 He came unto his own, and his own received him not. 12 But as many as received him, to them gave he power to become the sons of God, even to them that believe on his name : 13 Which were born, not of blood, nor of the will of the flesh, nor of the will of man, but of God. 14 And the Word was made flesh, and dwelt among us, (and we beheld his glory, the glory as of the only begotten of the Father), full of grace and truth.

15 John bare witness of him, and cried, saying, This was he of whom I spake, He that cometh after me is preferred before me : for he was before me. 16 And of his fulness have all we received, and grace for grace. 17 For the law was given by Moses, but grace and truth came by Jesus Christ. 18 No man hath seen God at any time ; the only begotten Son, which is in the bosom of the Father, he hath declared him.

EXPOSITION

This priceless Writing is in five parts as follows :—
PROLOGUE (i. 1–18). THE REVELATION OF GOD AS LIFE TO THE WORLD (i. 19 to xii. 50). THE REVELATION OF GOD AS LIGHT TO THE DISCIPLES (xiii. to xvii.). THE REVELATION OF GOD AS LOVE TO ALL (xviii. to xx.). EPILOGUE, xxi. Mark these divisions in your Bible, and master them.

Consider, I. THE PROLOGUE (i. 1-18), which looks *back*, and is in three distinct paragraphs.

1. *The Divine Revelation of the Word* (1-5); wherein is set forth His relation to *God* (1-2); to *Creation* (3); and to *Man* (4, 5). How exhaustless an unfolding! God has spoken only one WORD, but it includes the whole language. Nothing could more plainly declare Christ's Divinity, Infinity, and Eternity than these opening words: walk round them, enter into them, and lie down on them. He Who is God and Creator is also Redeemer, the *Life* and *Light* of men. The *darkness* did not, and cannot *overcome* the *Light* (5 R.V.).

2. *The Historic Manifestation of the Word* (6-13). He Who *was* from all eternity was manifested in *time* The Light was *revealed* (6-9); *rejected* (10-11); and *received* (12-13). Every one must do something with the Light. He Who made the world, and was in it, was not known by it (9). He came to His own world, and His own people, the Jews, received Him not (10, Gr.). Christ is at your door; have you let Him in? The Life has come, but the world is still dead: the Light has come, but it is still dark. Are you? Do you prefer a rushlight to the Redeemer? Remember, you may reject the Light, but you cannot quench it (4, 5).

3. *The Human Apprehension of the Word* (14-18). Here we have the witness of the *Apostles* (14); of the *Baptist* (15); and of the *Church* (16-18). Plunge into this ocean of truth. *Truth*, yes, and *grace* (14, 17): not the one without the cther. Do you prefer grace to truth? Will you to-day *receive of His fulness?* (16).

Thought: CHRISTIANITY IS BASED ON HISTORIC FACTS.

ST. JOHN i. 19-28
Title: TESTED BY TEMPTATION

19 And this is the record of John, when the Jews sent priests and Levites from Jerusalem to ask him,

Who art thou ? 20 And he confessed, and denied not ; but confessed, I am not the Christ. 21 And they asked him, What then ? Art thou Elias ? And he saith, I am not. Art thou that prophet ? And he answered, No. 22 Then said they unto him, Who art thou ? that we may give an answer to them that sent us. What sayest thou of thyself ? 23 He said, I am the voice of one crying in the wilderness, Make straight the way of the Lord, as said the prophet Esaias.

24 And they which were sent were of the Pharisees. 25 And they asked him, and said unto him, Why baptizest thou then, if thou be not that Christ, nor Elias, neither that prophet ? 26 John answered them, saying, I baptize with water : but there standeth one among you, whom ye know not ; 27 He it is, who coming after me is preferred before me, whose shoe's latchet I am not worthy to unloose. 28 These things were done in Bethabara beyond Jordan, where John was baptizing.

EXPOSITION

In verses 19–36, we have THE CONFESSION OF JOHN THE BAPTIST : 1. to *the Deputation from Jerusalem* (19–28) : 2. to *the Public* in general (29–34) ; 3. and to *two of his own Followers* (35, 36). Two things should impress us in this record.

First, the Baptist's *Disclaimer* (19–22), which is threefold. Members of the Sanhedrin, the chief Ecclesiastical Court of the Jews, were anxious to know who John was. From the questions they asked it is clear that they regarded him to be a very important person, and this fact presented both a temptation and an opportunity. The temptation was to accept their compliment, and claim to be either the *Messiah*, or *Elijah*, who was expected to reappear, or *the prophet* whom some identified with Jeremiah. John affirmed that he was neither, and his denials grew shorter, as though he were impatient of such questions. It is only small-souled men who are pretenders, who want people to think them to be what they are not. An honest person is content to be himself, or herself. Are you ?

The second thing to observe is, John's *Claim* (23–28). While he did not claim to be Christ, or Elijah, or Jeremiah, he did not deny himself. He *was* a very important person, and he knew it, and said so (23). He was the Messiah's herald, and the last of the O.T. prophets. It is as dishonest to deny what you are, as to claim to be what you are not. For Michael Angelo to say he could not chisel marble would not be modesty, but mockery. One can be true to Christ without being untrue to himself. John was " a burning and a shining light "; he was the last of the Old Testament prophets, and was, Jesus said, the greatest born of woman. Each of us can be great in humility, honesty, and loyalty. Are you ? There is no virtue in self-depreciation. Stand up like a man to what God has called you to be and to do.

Thought : *THERE IS A PLACE FOR ME IN THIS WORLD WHICH NO ONE ELSE CAN FILL.*

ST. JOHN i. 29-34

Title : *THE WITNESS OF JOHN THE BAPTIST*

29 The next day John seeth Jesus coming unto him, and saith, Behold the Lamb of God, which taketh away the sin of the world. **30** This is he of whom I said, After me cometh a man which is preferred before me : for he was before me. **31** And I knew him not : but that he should be made manifest to Israel, therefore am I come baptizing with water.

32 And John bare record, saying, I saw the Spirit descending from heaven like a dove, and it abode upon him. **33** And I knew him not ; but he that sent me to baptize with water, the same said unto me, Upon whom thou shalt see the Spirit descending, and remaining on him, the same is he which baptizeth with the Holy Ghost. **34** And I saw, and bare record that this is the Son of God.

EXPOSITION

The next part of the Baptist's Confession is to,
2. *The Public in general* (29–34). This paragraph is full of good things. John pointed men to Jesus, and he himself always got behind his Master (29, 30). Does every preacher do that ? Do you ? The slain Lamb was John's hope for men ; not education, social improvement and service, and certainly not ragtime and entertainment. Only the LAMB can *lift and carry away* (Gr.) the sin of the world. " *I knew Him not* " (33, cf. 26). Ignorance arises from various causes : in John's case from a want of revelation ; in the other case, from a want of regeneration.

" *Behold the Lamb* " (29) : " *I beheld the Spirit* " (32). After the Lamb, the Spirit : after conversion, consecration. Observe the Trinity in verse 33. Do not confuse Spirit-baptism and Water-baptism. The former is an inward grace ; the latter is an outward form, and either may be known without the other.

" *This is the Son of God* " (34). Follow the revelation of Christ in this chapter : *Word* (1), Light (7, 8), Son (18, 34, 49), *Lord* (23), *Jesus* (29), *Lamb* (29), *Rabbi* (38), *Messias* (41), *King of Israel* (49), *Son of man* (51). Do you worship and love Him ?

The third part of John's confession is to, 3. *Two of his own followers* (35, 36). These were John (the writer of this Gospel) and Andrew (40). An exact diary is kept of the events of a week : the days are definitely indicated : 1st (19–28), 2nd (29–34), 3rd (35–39), 4th (40–42), 5th (43–51), 6th (ii. 1–11), and following days (ii. 12). Do you keep a record of God's dealings with you ? The whole section 19–36, is a great record of *witness* ; a word which occurs in this Gospel nearly fifty times. We should tell all kinds of people, and at all times, all that we know about the Lord Jesus. The greatest work in the world is pointing and leading men to the Lamb of God.

Thought : **KEEP CLOSE BEHIND THE MASTER ALL THE DAY, AND ALL THE WAY.**

ST. JOHN i. 35-42

Title : THE CALL OF THE FIRST DISCIPLES

35 Again the next day after John stood, and two of his disciples : 36 And looking upon Jesus as he walked, he saith, Behold the Lamb of God ! 37 Then the two disciples heard him speak, and they followed Jesus. 38 Then Jesus turned, and saw them following, and saith unto them, What seek ye ? They said unto him, Rabbi, (which is to say, being interpreted), Master, where dwellest thou ? 39 He saith unto them, Come and see. They came and saw where he dwelt, and abode with him that day, for it was about the tenth hour.

40 One of the two which heard John speak, and followed him, was Andrew, Simon Peter's brother. 41 He first findeth his own brother Simon, and saith unto him, We have found the Messias, which is, being interpreted, the Christ. 42 And he brought him to Jesus. And when Jesus beheld him, he said, Thou art Simon the son of Jona : thou shalt be called Cephas, which is by interpretation, A stone.

EXPOSITION

Here is a wonderful lesson on *Soul-winning.* Five men attached themselves to Jesus : John and Andrew (37–40) ; Simon Peter (41, 42), Philip (43, 44), and Nathaniel (45–51). How did they come ? Well, the Baptist sent the first two (35, 36) ; Andrew brought Peter (42) ; Jesus sought out Philip (43), and Philip told Nathanael (45). In these various ways men reach Christ. Have you ever come to Him ? I do not ask if you are a Church member, or Sunday School teacher, or if you attend Communion, for one can do all that, and yet not be a Christian. Do you want to know how to become a Christian ? Read verse 12, on your knees.

Are you, who have come, *abiding* in Him (39 : read xv. 1–8) ? All Christians have not learned the secret of abiding. It is not *hanging on,* but *dwelling in.* If you have *come,* and are *abiding,* you will *serve* Him. Clear *vision* will lead to holy *passion* which will compel to dynamic *mission.* He who has truly found Christ, will find some one to bring to Him. These men did not change their craft: they still were *fishermen*. It is your present knowledge and ability which Christ would use. Embark on wider waters for a larger catch.

A good thing is worth telling and sharing. Perhaps it is always most difficult to bring one's own people to Christ (41), but it is gloriously worth while. Andrew never did a better day's work than when he brought Peter to Jesus. Think also of the obscure preacher who brought C. H. Spurgeon! and long before that, of the conversation of those women, which eventuated in Bunyan's conversion. No one is too obscure to bring another. Make up your mind to-day that you will not go to heaven empty-handed. Jesus began with five followers: how many has He to-day? (Rev. vii. 9-17).

Thought: *FOLLOW THE LAMB WHITHERSOEVER HE GOETH.*

ST. JOHN i. 43-51

Title: *FRUIT UNDER A FIG-TREE*

43 The day following Jesus would go forth into Galilee, and findeth Philip, and saith unto him, Follow me. **44** Now Philip was of Bethsaida, the city of Andrew and Peter. **45** Philip findeth Nathanael, and saith unto him, We have found him of whom Moses in the law, and the prophets, did write, Jesus of Nazareth, the son of Joseph. **46** And Nathanael said unto him, Can there any good thing come out of Nazareth? Philip saith unto him, Come and see.

47 Jesus saw Nathanael coming to him, and saith of him, Behold an Israelite indeed, in whom is no guile! **48** Nathanael saith unto him, Whence knowest thou me? Jesus answered and said unto him, Before that Philip called thee, when thou wast under the fig tree, I saw thee. **49** Nathanael answered and saith unto him, Rabbi, thou art the Son of God; thou art the King of Israel. **50** Jesus answered and said unto him, Because I said unto thee, I saw thee under the fig tree, believest thou?

thou shalt see greater things than these. 51 And he saith unto him, Verily, verily, I say unto you, Hereafter ye shall see heaven open, and the angels of God ascending and descending upon the Son of man.

EXPOSITION

This is a chapter of great discoveries. John finds Jesus, Andrew finds Peter, Jesus finds Philip, and Philip finds Nathanael; and great finding it is ! Whenever Jesus " *was minded to go forth* " (43), it was because He had something in His mind, and, in this instance, it was Nathanael, who is to be identified with Bartholomew the Apostle. The Greek form of the name, *Theodore*, means *God's gift*, and truly Jesus was the gift of God to him, but he had to come, before he could receive (46).

By Philip's " *we have found Him,*" Jesus, previous search is implied, and we may assume also that Nathanael had been a companion in the search. So is it proved again that " *they that seek Me early shall find Me.*"

Jesus came and is ever coming from unexpected quarters (46). Nathanael could not believe that the Messiah would appear from among a despised people, in a despised town, in a despised province in the North. Would He not arise in Jerusalem, from Zion the City of God ? No ! He was born, and lived, and died outside Jerusalem. For thirty years of His short life he lived and worked in the little town which is not even named in the Old Testament.

How wise was Philip's answer to his friend's enquiry, " *Come and see.*" That is the true solution of religious doubts. Arguing is of no use. Invite men and women to test out for themselves the Gospel, and experience will always authenticate revelation. You should observe the references here to Jacob's experiences in Genesis, in verse 47, to Genesis xxxii, and in verse 51, to Genesis xxviii. Nathanael has already a spiritual experience, and something better awaits him. Are you expecting more ?

Nathanael had a progressive mind and heart; he lived up to his light, and when he got more light he lived still higher up (48, 49). Here he makes great strides in faith, gladly acknowledging Jesus' divine origin and human sovereignty, "*Son of God*," and "*King of Israel*." When He is the King of *Israel*, it is good to be an *Israelite* (49, 47). When He is the *Christ* of God, it is good to be a *Christian*. Both Nathanael and Augustine were found by Christ *under a fig tree* (50). See the "*Confessions*," viii. 12, 28.

There are always "*greater things*" (50) for those who love God. For such, the best is never behind. Why should we live a poor withered life when *heaven is open*, and *angelic messengers* are in continuous communication with our world? *Why*?

Thought: *ALL WHO HAVE BEEN FOUND SHOULD BECOME FINDERS.*

ST. JOHN ii. 1-12

Title: *JESUS AT A WEDDING*

1 And the third day there was a marriage in Cana of Galilee ; and the mother of Jesus was there : 2 And both Jesus was called, and his disciples, to the marriage. 3 And when they wanted wine, the mother of Jesus saith unto him, They have no wine. 4 Jesus saith unto her, Woman, what have I to do with thee ? mine hour is not yet come. 5 His mother saith unto the servants, Whatsoever he saith unto you, do it.

6 And there were set there six waterpots of stone, after the manner of the purifying of the Jews, containing two or three firkins apiece. 7 Jesus saith unto them, Fill the waterpots with water. And they filled them up to the brim. 8 And he saith unto them, Draw out now, and bear unto the governor of the feast. And they bare it. 9 When the ruler of the feast had tasted the water that was made wine; and knew not whence it was : (but the servants which drew the water knew ;) the governor of the feast called the bridegroom, 10 And saith unto him, Every man at the beginning doth set

forth good wine : and when men have well drunk, then that which is worse : but thou hast kept the good wine until now. 11 This beginning of miracles did Jesus in Cana of Galilee, and manifested forth his glory ; and his disciples believed on him. 12 After this he went down to Capernaum, he, and his mother, and his brethren, and his disciples : and they continued there not many days.

EXPOSITION

It is impressive to read this story with ch. i. 1–5. He Who created the Universe attended a wedding : the eternal Son of God was a guest at a feast. Christ has been called a " pale Galilean," but never was there in the world a more joyful person ; under the shadow of the Cross He spoke more of joy than ever He had done before. Early in His matchless ministry He accepted an invitation to a domestic social function.

Do you look for Christ only in the shadows, only among the tombs ? Learn from our portion that He is not a joy-killer, but a joy-bringer : He is not for death-beds only, but also for dinners. We call upon Him to help us in our pains, but we need Him also to sanctify our pleasures. A Christless wedding is a failure from the start. People who get married without the Master are asking for trouble.

This would have been a dry-jar wedding if Jesus had not been there. His reply to His mother was firm but respectful. Jesus worked by God's clock ; He never did anything before the appointed time (4). Whenever His hour comes we should be ready to do His bidding (5), whatever He commands. Does He find you willing and ready ?

Only the Master can work the miracle (11), but we must fill the water-pots (7). We cannot do His work, and He will not do ours.

"*This beginning of miracles*" was surely symbolic of two dispensations, Law and Grace ; and of the

two stages of one Divine revelation, the water representing Judaism, and the wine, Christianity. Remember, the wine was *after* the water, *from* it, and *better* than it. Have you invited Jesus Christ to your next party? Would His presence spoil your plans?
Thought: WHERE JESUS IS THERE IS JOY.

ST. JOHN ii. 13-25

Title: PEOPLE WHO DISAPPOINTED THE MASTER

13 And the Jews' passover was at hand, and Jesus went up to Jerusalem. 14 And found in the temple those that sold oxen and sheep and doves, and the changers of money sitting: 15 And when he had made a scourge of small cords, he drove them all out of the temple, and the sheep, and the oxen; and poured out the changers' money, and overthrew the tables; 16 And said unto them that sold doves, Take these things hence; make not my Father's house an house of merchandise. 17 And his disciples remembered that it was written, the zeal of thine house hath eaten me up. 18 Then answered the Jews and said unto him, What sign shewest thou unto us, seeing that thou doest these things? 19 Jesus answered and said unto them, Destroy this temple, and in three days I will raise it up. 20 Then said the Jews, Forty and six years was this temple in building, and wilt thou rear it up in three days? 21 But he spake of the temple of his body. 22 When therefore he was risen from the dead, his disciples remembered that he had said this unto them: and they believed the scripture, and the word which Jesus had said.

23 Now when he was in Jerusalem at the passover, in the feast day, many believed in his name, when they saw the miracles which he did. 24 But Jesus did not commit himself unto them, because he knew all men. 25 And needed not that any should testify of man: for he knew what was in man.

EXPOSITION

There are here three short but weighty lessons.

1. JESUS CLEANSES THE TEMPLE (13–17). It should astonish us that the *Temple* needed and needs

cleansing, yet so it was and is. When a man or a family join a church for the trade it is likely to bring their way, they identify themselves with these people whom Jesus lashed. Christ is interested in commerce, but He wants us to keep it out of Church. Do you sing in the choir for the fee you can get? If Jesus were here He would drive you out. Do you preach to make a living? Then you are nearer Judas than Jesus. Of course a preacher must live, but if his salary is with him the determining factor, he is a hireling and not a shepherd. Have you a holy zeal for God's house—your body, your church, and the universal spiritual Temple?

2. JESUS ANTICIPATES HIS DEATH (18–22). It is noteworthy how people using the same language may mean totally different things. Illustration of this we have in chapter iv, about *water*; in chapter iii, about *birth*; and here, about *temple*. The Jews were thinking of the stone structure, but Jesus, of His own body. Contemplate the *impotence* of men—taking forty-six years to put up that building—and the *omnipotence* of Christ—raising His dead body from the grave after it had lain there for three days! Verse 22 teaches us that there are some things which can be fully understood only in the light of fulfilment, though, no doubt, we might better understand them before.

3. JESUS' UNERRING INSIGHT (23–25). The force of the Greek here is, "*they trusted Him, but He did not trust them.*" But why? Because He *knew* them. Their interest was in what He was doing, and not in Himself (23); therefore He had no faith in their faith. Jesus' attitude and action towards us are determined by His infallible knowledge of us.

Thought: *CHRIST TRUSTS HIMSELF TO THOSE WHO TRUST HIM.*

ST. JOHN iii. 1-13
Title: *LIFE FROM ABOVE*

1 There was a man of the Pharisees, named Nicodemus, a ruler of the Jews: 2 The same came

to Jesus by night, and said unto him, Rabbi, we know that thou art a teacher come from God : for no man can do these miracles that thou doest, except God be with him.

3 Jesus answered and said unto him, Verily, verily, I say unto thee, Except a man be born again, he cannot see the kingdom of God.

4 Nicodemus saith unto him, How can a man be born when he is old ? can he enter the second time into his mother's womb, and be born ?

5 Jesus answered, Verily, verily, I say unto thee, Except a man be born of water and of the Spirit, he cannot enter into the kingdom of God. 6 That which is born of the flesh is flesh ; and that which is born of the Spirit is spirit. 7 Marvel not that I said unto thee, Ye must be born again. 8 The wind bloweth where it listeth, and thou hearest the sound thereof, but canst not tell whence it cometh, and whither it goeth : so is every one that is born of the Spirit.

9 Nicodemus answered and said unto him, How can these things be ?

10 Jesus answered and said unto him, Art thou a master of Israel, and knowest not these things ? 11 Verily, verily, I say unto thee, We speak that we do know, and testify that we have seen ; and ye receive not our witness. 12 If I have told you earthly things, and ye believe not, how shall ye believe, if I tell you of heavenly things ? 13 And no man hath ascended up to heaven, but he that came down from heaven, even the Son of man which is in heaven.

EXPOSITION

For a minute or two do a bit of survey work. In chapters i, ii, CHRIST THE DIVINE LIFE HAS BEEN *Announced*, by the witness of the Baptist, of the first Disciples, and of Nature. In chapters, v.–xii, we shall see THE LIFE *Antagonized* ; but between these, let us contemplate THE LIFE *Acknowledged*, chapters iii.–iv. ; and by three types of persons ; a Pharisee and member of the Sanhedrin (iii. 1–21) ; a Samaritan woman (iv. 1–42) ; and a Herodian courtier (iv. 43–54). These are found in the three parts of

Palestine—Judea, Samaria, and Galilee; and three avenues of approach to the soul are here revealed—by the mind, the conscience, and the heart. This division of the Gospel is, therefore, in scope, universal, representative, and comprehensive.

All the history of NICODEMUS is in this Gospel: (a) HIS DESIRE FOR CHRIST (iii. 1–21); (b) His DEFENCE OF CHRIST (vii. 45–52); and (c) His DEVOTION TO CHRIST (xix. 38–42. Our portion reveals THE NECESSITY OF REGENERATION. Nicodemus was a *ruler* but nevertheless he needed a *redeemer*. He thought well of Jesus (2), but not well enough (13). Every Institution has its terms of admission, then why not the Church? Christ here lays down the basic condition of membership, "*ye must be born again.*" There is no other way. Eternal life is the hall-mark of the subjects of this Kingdom.

The *wind* and the *Spirit*, as to their action, are alike in that they are *free, manifest, mysterious,* and *powerful* (8). Both Nicodemus and Jesus asked " how ? " (4, 9, 12). The old scholar came to the young Saviour. What began as a general discussion, Jesus soon turned to a personal application. Are you saved? Christ is asking of you not compliments, but contrition and consecration. The *new birth* is a profound mystery, but it is also an indisputable fact. Psychologists and evolutionists may doubt or deny it, but the facts are against them when they are against this fact. Are you demonstrating this truth?

Thought: DOUBT CAN BE HONEST AND REVERENT (iv. 9).

ST. JOHN iii. 14-24

Title: TO THE RIGHT AND TO THE LEFT

14 And as Moses lifted up the serpent in the wilderness, even so must the Son of man be lifted up: 15 That whosoever believeth in him should not perish, but have eternal life. 16 For God so loved the world, that he gave his only begotten Son, that whosoever believeth in him should not perish

but have everlasting life. 17 For God sent not his Son into the world to condemn the world ; but that the world through him might be saved.

18 He that believeth on him is not condemned : but he that believeth not is condemned already, because he hath not believed in the name of the only begotten Son of God. 19 And this is the condemnation, that light is come into the world, and men loved darkness rather than light, because their deeds were evil. 20 For every one that doeth evil hateth the light, neither cometh to the light, lest his deeds should be reproved. 21 But he that doeth truth cometh to the light, that his deeds may be made manifest, that they are wrought in God.

22 After these things came Jesus and his disciples into the land of Judæa ; and there he tarried with them, and baptized. 23 And John also was baptizing in Ænon near to Salim, because there was much water there : and they came, and were baptized. 24 For John was not yet cast into prison.

EXPOSITION

There is good reason for thinking that the conversation between Jesus and Nicodemus ends at verse 15, and that verses 16–21, are the reflections of the Evangelist. The expressions *" only-begotten Son "* (never used by Jesus Himself) ; *" believeth on the name "* ; *" to do truth "* ; and the tenses in verse 19b, *" loved "* and *" were,"* all point to this conclusion.

In verse 14 is a new interpretation of a well-known incident in Jewish history. *" Lifted up "* is used three times in this Gospel of Christ and His Cross (14 ; viii. 28 ; xii. 32). To *perish* or to have *eternal life*, these are the alternatives (16). *Eternal*, when associated with *life*, refers quite as much to the *quality* of the life as to its duration.

Have you ever noticed that the word *Gospel* occurs in the classic 16th verse ? the initial letters of six of its words. " God so loved the world, that He gave His Only-begotten Son, that whosoever believeth on Him should not Perish, but have Everlasting Life." Think of this love of God as to its Nature, *" so "* ; its Scope, *" the world . . ."* ;

its Proof, "*He gave*"; its Freeness, "*whosoever*"; and its Effect, "*everlasting life.*"

Why did God send His Son into the world? (17). *Condemnation* and *justification* are conditioned on *faith* (18). John is the Apostle of sharp antitheses: death and life (16); belief and unbelief (18); light and darkness (19); love and hate (19, 20); doing evil and doing truth (20, 21). The Gospel message knows no neutrality. Every one must be either *for* or *against* Jesus Christ, and not to be for Him is to be against Him. There are only two *ways*, and only two *destinies*. In which way are you, and for which goal are you heading? Enough is revealed in this portion to *sink* or *save* the world. All the Gospel is truth, but all truth is not the Gospel.

Thought: *BY HIS UPLIFTING ARE WE LIFTED UP.*

ST. JOHN iii. 25-36

Title: *THE CONCLUSION OF A GREAT TESTIMONY*

25 Then there arose a question between some of John's disciples and the Jews about purifying, 26 And they came unto John, and said unto him. Rabbi, he that was with thee beyond Jordan, to whom thou barest witness, behold, the same baptizeth, and all men come to him.

27 John answered and said, A man can receive nothing, except it be given him from heaven. 28 Ye yourselves bear me witness, that I said, I am not the Christ, but that I am sent before him. 29 He that hath the bride is the bridegroom: but the friend of the bridegroom, which standeth and heareth him, rejoiceth greatly because of the bridegroom's voice: this my joy therefore is fulfilled. 30 He must increase, but I must decrease.

31 He that cometh from above is above all: he that is of the earth is earthly, and speaketh of the earth: he that cometh from heaven is above all. 32 And what he hath seen and heard, that he testifieth; and no man receiveth his testimony. 33 He

that hath received his testimony hath set to his seal that God is true. 34 For he whom God hath sent speaketh the words of God : for God giveth not the Spirit by measure unto him. 35 The Father loveth the Son, and hath given all things into his hand. 36 He that believeth on the Son hath everlasting life : and he that believeth not the Son shall not see life ; but the wrath of God abideth on him.

EXPOSITION

In verses 22-30, we hear the last of John the Baptist. He closes as he commenced, he was loyal to the last. John and Jesus' disciples were both baptizing (22, 23 ; and iv. 1, 2). This led the Jews to start a controversy (25, 26) : they were very good at that, as a lot of people are. There would be less debate if everybody did his own thinking ; but numberless people " put out " their thinking, as they do their washing. Well, John soon silenced their cavil. What, in effect, he said was, "*I am Jesus' friend, not His rival.*" He confirms his first testimony (28 : and chap. i). Do you bear a consistent witness ?

John's business was to bring the bride and the bridegroom together ; that done, his work was done ; "*this my joy has been fulfilled*" (29). How great a thing it will be if, at last, you and I can say, "*we have done what God sent us into the world to do.*" John's was unselfish success. " HE MUST INCREASE, BUT I MUST DECREASE " (30). Could one finish his life's task more nobly than that ? Selfish success is utter failure, but to magnify Christ is to " win through " gloriously. The patron is surely greater than the protégé, and the head greater than the hand !

Verses 31-36 are considered by many to be the Evangelist's, not the Baptist's words, and not without good reason. The Apostle John is eminently theological in his reflections, and mystical. Note two things only in these verses : first, that *the Word of God* (i. 1) *speaks the words of God* (34) ; and second, that the Father Who loves Him, *has given all things into His hand.* Do you really believe that *all things* are in the hands of the Lord Jesus ? Then you will have no panic, and no unnerving fear.

Thought : LOVE AND LOYALTY ARE TWIN SISTERS.

ST. JOHN iv. 1-14

Title : METHOD IN SOUL WINNING

1 When therefore the Lord knew how the Pharisees had heard that Jesus made and baptized more disciples than John, 2 (Though Jesus himself baptized not, but his disciples), 3 He left Judæa, and departed again into Galilee. 4 And he must needs go through Samaria.

5 Then cometh he to a city of Samaria, which is called Sychar, near to the parcel of ground that Jacob gave to his son Joseph. 6 Now Jacob's well was there. Jesus therefore, being wearied with his journey, sat thus on the well : and it was about the sixth hour.

7 There cometh a woman of Samaria to draw water ; Jesus saith unto her, Give me to drink. 8 (For his disciples were gone away unto the city to buy meat).

9 Then saith the woman of Samaria unto him, How is it that thou, being a Jew, askest drink of me, which am a woman of Samaria (for the Jews have no dealings with the Samaritans)?

10 Jesus answered and said unto her, If thou knewest the gift of God, and who it is that saith to thee, Give me to drink ; thou wouldest have asked of him, and he would have given thee living water.

11 The woman saith unto him, Sir, thou hast nothing to draw with, and the well is deep : from whence then hast thou that living water ? 12 Art thou greater than our father Jacob, which gave us the well, and drank thereof himself, and his children, and his cattle ?

13 Jesus answered and said unto her, Whosoever drinketh of this water shall thirst again : 14 But whosoever drinketh of the water that I shall give

him shall never thirst : but the water that I shall give him shall be in him a well of water springing up into everlasting life.

EXPOSITION

Here is a detailed superb illustration of how Christ dealt with souls, and of the method whereby we too may reach them. The great underlying principle is, *find a point of contact with the one whom you would win.* Follow this out in the present instance. From start to finish there are seven stages in this capture, two of which we consider now.

1. THE PREPARATION (1–6). This leads up to the main story, and is full of practical interest. Mark a few points. Verse 1. "*The Lord.*" During His earthly sojourn He was known and spoken of as *Jesus*, but John, writing at the close of the first century, rightly calls Him *Lord*. Verse 2. A note of the Evangelist's, correcting a rumour. The Master of the house does not do the porter's work. Verse 4. The *necessity* here referred to was partly geographical, but predominently spiritual. There was another route from Judea to Galilee, which some took for the reason stated in verse 9 ; but Jesus' purpose to bless, cuts through all prejudice. Verse 6. "*Well,*" that is *spring*, or *fountain* as in verse 14 ; but in verses 11, 12, it is *well*, or *cistern* ; this is an important distinction. "*The sixth hour*," that is 12 o'noon, the hottest hour of the day. Jesus was *tired* and sat down to rest ; but He was never too tired to do good. Place, time, circumstances, all prepare for the great event.

2. THE APPROACH (7–15). Mark how naturally the conversation opens up. The Lord of Glory asks an adultress for a drink of water. Why ? Incidentally because He was thirsty, but principally because He wanted to give her a draught of "*living water.*" *Thirst and water*, therefore, are the points of contact (10, 13, 14). "*If thou hadst known*" (10, cf. Matt. xii. 7). Think of the things you would and would not have thought, and said, and done if only you had known, what you might well have known. Ignorance

of the things that matter most is folly, and weakness, and a curse. Slowly Jesus is leading this woman to God. Let us pray for a measure of His patience.

Thought : *WHY BE WEAK FOR WANT OF WATER WHEN YOUR SOUL MAY BE A WELL ?*

ST. JOHN iv. 15-30

Title : *SPIRITUAL STRATEGY*

15 The woman saith unto him, Sir, give me this water, that I thirst not, neither come hither to draw.

16 Jesus saith unto her, Go, call thy husband, and come hither.

17 The woman answered and said, I have no husband.

Jesus said unto her, Thou hast well said, I have no husband ; 18 For thou hast had five husbands ; and he whom thou now hast is not thy husband : in that saidst thou truly.

19 The woman saith unto him, Sir, I perceive that thou art a prophet. 20 Our fathers worshipped in this mountain ; and ye say, that in Jerusalem is the place where men ought to worship.

21 Jesus saith unto her, Woman, believe me, the hour cometh, when ye shall neither in this mountain, nor yet at Jerusalem, worship the Father. 22 Ye worship ye know not what : we know what we worship : for salvation is of the Jews. 23 But the hour cometh, and now is, when the true worshippers shall worship the Father in spirit and in truth : for the Father seeketh such to worship him. 24 God is a Spirit : and they that worship him must worship him in spirit and in truth.

25 The woman saith unto him, I know that Messias cometh, which is called Christ : when he is come, he will tell us all things.

26 Jesus saith unto her, I that speak unto thee am he.

17 And upon this came his disciples, and marvelled that he talked with the woman : yet no man said, What seekest thou ? or, Why talkest thou with her ?

28 The woman then left her waterpot, and went her way into the city, and saith to the men, 29 Come see a man, which told me all things that ever I did: is not this the Christ ? 30 Then they went out of the city, and came unto him.

EXPOSITION

See the two points in the preceding portion. In Christ's method to win this soul, there is in the third place, 3. THE ASSAULT (16–18). The moment had now come when a raid must be made upon this woman's conscience. Nicodemus' difficulty was *intellectual* ; this woman's was *moral* ; both needed the gospel, but both were not reached in the same way. Note the suddenness and directness of Jesus' attack : He stormed the fort with vigour. That is the only hope in many a case : some people must be awakened to realities by means of surprise.

Jesus said " *go . . . and come* " (16) : He was not sending her away. Let us not imagine this woman to be worse than she was ; she had been married to the five men, but not to the sixth ; at a point in her life there was a moral breakdown. I wonder how that came about ! Beware !

4. THE ADVANCE (19–24). The woman, by her reply to Jesus, admitted her guilt : an innocent person would not have said what is recorded in verse 19. But her guilt admitted, she wishes to dodge the matter, and so starts an argument ; but the shaft has found a lodgment. Mark the growth of Christ upon this woman : *Jew* (9) ; *Sir* (11) ; *Prophet* (19) ; *the Christ* (29). Is Christ becoming more and more to *you* ? Have *you* a pet sin in your life ? A man may be quite willing to discuss the outer matters of religion, and yet be quite unwilling to be judged by its inner truth. Is that true of you ?

5. THE CAPTURE (25, 26). Here the conversation ends, because the goal has been reached. Jesus first revealed this woman to herself, and then, Himself to her. That is always the way : it is only the sick who need a physician, only the sinner who needs a

Saviour. Jesus here plainly claims to be the promised Messiah (26).

6. THE WITNESS (27–30). Surely the most proper and natural thing for a saved soul to do, is to tell some one else of the Saviour. Have you done that?

Thought: *THERE IS NOT A HUMAN BEING WHO IS NOT WORTH WINNING.*

ST. JOHN iv. 31-42

Title: *SUSTAINING SERVICE*

31 In the meanwhile his disciples prayed him, saying, Master, eat.
32 But he said unto them, I have meat to eat that ye know not of.
33 Therefore said the disciples one to another, Hath any man brought him ought to eat?
34 Jesus saith unto them, My meat is to do the will of him that sent me, and to finish his work. 35 Say not ye, There are yet four months, and then cometh harvest? behold, I say unto you, Lift up your eyes, and look on the fields: for they are white already to harvest. 36 And he that reapeth receiveth wages, and gathereth fruit unto life eternal; that both he that soweth and he that reapeth may rejoice together. 37 And herein is that saying true, One soweth, and another reapeth. 38 I sent you to reap that whereon ye bestowed no labour: other men laboured, and ye are entered into their labours.

39 And many of the Samaritans of that city believed on him for the saying of the woman, which testified, He told me all that ever I did. 40 So when the Samaritans were come unto him, they besought him that he would tarry with them and he abode there two days. 41 And many more believed because of his own word: 42 And said unto the woman, Now we believe, not because of thy saying: for we have heard him ourselves, and know that this is indeed the Christ, the Saviour of the world.

EXPOSITION

Review the six points of the preceding verses of this chapter. We now come to the seventh and last in this story: 7. THE CONSEQUENCES (31–42). There are two great paragraphs here.

(i) *Jesus' lesson on Sowing and Reaping* (31–38). Mark His absorbing enthusiasm in soul-winning (31–34). Some people are more anxious about suppers than souls, and would rather dine than seek a degenerate. That was not the Lord Jesus' case: soul-seeking and soul-saving were to Him nourishment (32). Have you ever felt like that? The Master had a great consciousness of vocation, and a flaming ambition to complete His task. How great is the thrill of worthy accomplishment! Let your pleasure and your profit go hand in hand as you carry out the programme which God has made for you (34).

And now, out of His action comes a lesson (35–38). Contemplate the great truths here taught—that there is a harvest waiting to be reaped (35); that not only are we called to sow what others will reap, but also to reap what others have sown (37, 38); that both sower and reaper will meet at the granary in the glory (36). Let us remember more what they who went before us have done. Our churches are products of men and women whose footprints across the pages of Church history can be traced by blood.

Our second paragraph tells of (ii) *The Verification of Experience* (39–42). Why do you believe? Because some one has borne a testimony, or because you have felt? Another person's faith will not save you; *you* must believe. *Assent* and *consent* are not the same. Assent comes of knowing Christ *mediately* (39), but consent, by knowing Him *immediately* (42). Nothing will do but direct contact with the Saviour Himself, "*the Saviour of the world.*"

Thought: *THERE'S A FIELD AWAITING MY SICKLE TO-DAY.*

ST. JOHN iv. 43–54

Title: *A NOBLE NOBLEMAN ENNOBLED*

43 Now after two days he departed thence, and went into Galilee. 44 For Jesus himself testified,

that a prophet hath no honour in his own country.
45 Then when he was come into Galilee, the Galilæans received him, having seen all the things that he did at Jerusalem at the feast ; for they also went unto the feast.

46 So Jesus came again into Cana of Galilee, where he made the water wine. And there was a certain nobleman, whose son was sick at Capernaum. 47 When he heard that Jesus was come out of Judea into Galilee, he went unto him, and besought him that he would come down, and heal his son ; for he was at the point of death.

48 Then said Jesus unto him, Except ye see signs and wonders, ye will not believe.

49 The nobleman saith unto him, Sir, come down ere my child die.

50 Jesus saith unto him, Go thy way : thy son liveth. And the man believed the word that Jesus had spoken unto him, and he went his way.

51 And as he was now going down, his servants met him, and told him, saying, Thy son liveth.
52 Then enquired he of them the hour when he began to amend. And they said unto him, Yesterday at the seventh hour the fever left him. 53 So the father knew that it was at the same hour, in the which Jesus said unto him, Thy son liveth ; and himself believed, and his whole house.

54 This is again the second miracle that Jesus did, when he was come out of Judæa into Galilee.

EXPOSITION

1. It is a thousand pities that so many folks have to go from home to be appreciated (43–45), yet so it is. Many a preacher is more used in other pulpits than in his own ; and the reason, not infrequently, is to be found in the pew—his own people do not come with the expectation and give him the encouragement which he meets with abroad. " It is a shame to support a stranger, and starve a son."

2. The story of this nobleman is very illuminating (46–53), for it is a lesson in *the development of faith*. Three times his faith comes into view ; when he came to Jesus he was exercising faith (47) ; when Jesus said his son was healed, he believed (50) ; and when

he got home again he believed still more (53). Faith is not like a brick, but like a plant ; it is as a grain that grows, first the blade, then the ear, then the full corn in the ear. Such was this man's faith ; it came to maturity. Has the development of your faith been arrested ? How ? Why ?

This man came to Jesus on behalf of his sick son. Perhaps you have children who will not come to the Saviour for themselves ; see, then, that you come to Him for them. Many a son and daughter has been saved from disaster and death because a father or mother came to Jesus on their knees.

3. With verse 54, a great division of this Gospel ends. Jesus has been at work in *Judea, Samaria,* and *Galilee* and we have seen Him giving life to a *man*, a *woman*, and a *child*. His first miracle was wrought at a marriage, and His second, in a house of mourning. His work sweeps the whole horizon between happiness and hopelessness ; if it did not, He could not be the Saviour of the world. The Lord has a heart for laughter and tears ; He meets us in the sunshine, and in the shadows. He is the Lord of the whole life : He will guard our gladness, and transfigure our tears. Have you found Him to be all that to you ?

Thought : " *I CLIMB THE RAINBOW THROUGH THE RAIN.*"

ST. JOHN v. 1-14

Title : OMNIPOTENCE MEETS IMPOTENCE

1 After this there was a feast of the Jews ; and Jesus went up to Jerusalem. 2 Now there is at Jerusalem by the sheep market a pool, which is called in the Hebrew tongue Bethesda, having five porches. 3 In these lay a great multitude of impotent folk, of blind, halt, withered, waiting for the moving of the water. 4 For an angel went down at a certain season into the pool, and troubled the water: whosoever then first after the troubling of the water stepped in was made whole of whatsoever disease he had.

5 And a certain man was there, which had an

infirmity thirty and eight years. 6 When Jesus saw him lie, and knew that he had been now a long time in that case, he saith unto him, Wilt thou be made whole?

7 The impotent man answered him, Sir, I have no man, when the water is troubled, to put me into the pool : but while I am coming, another steppeth down before me.

8 Jesus saith unto him, Rise, take up thy bed, and walk. 9 And immediately the man was made whole, and took up his bed, and walked : and on the same day was the sabbath.

10 The Jews therefore said unto him that was cured, It is the sabbath day : it is not lawful for thee to carry thy bed. 11 He answered them, He that made me whole, the same said unto me, Take up thy bed, and walk. 12 Then asked they him, What man is that which said unto thee, Take up thy bed, and walk ? 13 And he that was healed wist not who it was : for Jesus had conveyed himself away, a multitude being in that place.

14 Afterward Jesus findeth him in the temple, and said unto him, Behold, thou art made whole : sin no more, lest a worse thing come unto thee.

EXPOSITION

Let us divide this chapter into three parts, and call them the Sign, the Sequel, and the Sermon.

1. THE SIGN (1-9). Watering places did not begin with Buxton, and Droitwich, and Harrogate ; there was one at Jerusalem over 1,900 years ago. It is astonishing how careful people are of their bodies, and careless of their souls ; they take their bodies to the springs, and leave their souls by the sewer. This man had been impotent for thirty-eight years (5), and evidently his infirmity was due to his sin (14). Contrast ix. 1-3. Jesus had a way of finding out hard cases ; the great Physician occupied Himself more with heart disease than with headache. The Master sought out this meeting-place of pain, and dealt with the worst case there.

The greatest of all blessings is not forced upon us : we are consulted, and must give our consent (6). Many still are looking to a *pool* instead of resorting to the *physician* (7) ; are trusting *ritual*, and passing by the *Redeemer*. Are you ? The man who desires Christ need wait for no one—come right along just now (7), and hear Him say, " *Rise—take—walk* " (8) ; and believe that always *His commands are His enablings* (9).

2. THE SEQUEL (10-18) ; What follows is more than disappointing. We have no reason to expect much of these *Jews* (18), but certainly we expected more of the healed man, who, however, betrayed his Benefactor (13, 15). How base human nature can be ! What was the complaint ? That Jesus had healed a man on the Sabbath. But surely there was no better day in the week for such an act ! Beware lest, while being as orthodox as heaven about the Sabbath, you be as heterodox as hell about salvation. Do you prefer *convention* to *conversion* ? What is the good of a system which shackles the Saviour ? The Jews unwittingly were true commentators (18).

Thought : *THERE IS WORK WHICH IS REST ; AND THERE IS REST WHICH IS RUST* (17).

ST. JOHN v. 15-29

Title : *AN UNVEILING OF COMING JUDGMENT*

15 The man departed, and told the Jews that it was Jesus, which had made him whole. 16 And therefore did the Jews persecute Jesus, and sought to slay him, because he had done these things on the sabbath day.

17 But Jesus answered them, My Father worketh hitherto, and I work.

18 Therefore the Jews sought the more to kill him, because he not only had broken the sabbath, but said also that God was his Father, making himself equal with God.

19 Then answered Jesus and said unto them, Verily, verily, I say unto you, The Son can do nothing of himself, but what he seeth the Father do : for what things soever he doeth, these also doeth the Son likewise. 20 For the Father loveth the Son, and sheweth him all things that himself doeth : and

he will shew him greater works than these, that ye may marvel. 21 For as the Father raiseth up the dead, and quickeneth them ; even so the Son quickeneth whom he will. 22 For the Father judgeth no man, but hath committed all judgment unto the Son : 23 That all men should honour the Son, even as they honour the Father, He that honoureth not the Son honoureth not the Father which hath sent him.

24 Verily, verily, I say unto you, He that heareth my word, and believeth on him that sent me, hath everlasting life, and shall not come into condemnation : but is passed from death unto life. 25 Verily, verily, I say unto you, The hour is coming, and now is, when the dead shall hear the voice of the Son of God ; and they that hear shall live. 26 For as the Father hath life in himself ; so hath he given to the Son to have life in himself. 27 And hath given him authority to execute judgment also, because he is the Son of man.

28 Marvel not at this : for the hour is coming, in the which all that are in the graves shall hear his voice. 29 And shall come forth ; they that have done good, unto the resurrection of life : and they that have done evil, unto the resurrection of damnation.

EXPOSITION

Glance at the two points in the preceding portion and mark now :—

3. THE SERMON (19-37), which arises out of the SIGN (1-9), and the SEQUEL (10-18). The Sermon appears to fall into two parts. In the first, the Lord bears witness to Himself, and in the second, He calls other witnesses.

(i) *Christ's Witness to Himself* (19-29). The Jews had just questioned the right of Jesus to heal on the Sabbath, and challenged His claim to be equal with God (10, 18). In reply, He declares, first, the *ground* of His authority and claim (19, 20), and then, the *extent* of it (21-29). You will observe that here a profounder note is struck than we have heard before : these are the " *heavenly things* " of iii. 12.

There is no room in this discourse for Unitarianism. *The FATHER and the SON are one, and they share their powers and honours; albeit, providentially and dispensationally, the* SON *is subject to the* FATHER (19-23). Read these verses again, with this sentence of exposition. The reality and solemnity of what Jesus says is intimated by the thrice repeated " *Verily, verily* " (19, 24, 25). In what follows (24-29), Christ claims to be two things, *Life-giver* and *Judge*.

Verse 24 is another of the verses which Luther called " little Bibles," that is, verses which contain the whole Gospel (cf. iii. 16; Isaiah xlv. 21, 22). How momentous is the revelation of *Christ Himself*, and of *the Future* in these verses! He is the *Son of God* (25), and the *Son of Man* also (27), and it is as the GOD-MAN that He will judge the world. Both the saved and the unsaved are to be resurrected and judged, and destiny will be determined by character (28, 29). Do not imagine that it does not matter how you live and die. Our age is as sceptical of coming Judgment as was Noah's age, but it came then, and will come again. Ask yourself two questions: " What do I think of Christ? " " What does Christ think of me? "

Thought: BECAUSE GOD IS JUST, A JUDGMENT-DAY IS CERTAIN.

ST. JOHN v. 30-47

Title: WITNESSES TO CHRIST

30 I can of mine own self do nothing: as I hear, I judge: and my judgment is just; because I seek not mine own will, but the will of the Father which hath sent me. 31 If I bear witness of myself, my witness is not true. 32 There is another that beareth witness of me; and I know that the witness which he witnesseth of me is true.

33 Ye sent unto John, and he bare witness unto the truth. 34 But I receive not testimony from man: but these things I say, that ye might be saved. 35 He was a burning and a shining light: and ye were willing for a season to rejoice in his light.

36 But I have greater witness than that of John: for the works which the Father hath given me to

finish, the same works that I do, bear witness of me, that the Father hath sent me. 37 And the Father himself, which hath sent me, hath borne witness of me. Ye have neither heard his voice at any time, nor seen his shape. 38 And ye have not his word abiding in you : for whom he hath sent, him ye believe not.

39 Search the scriptures ; for in them ye think ye have eternal life : and they are they which testify of me. 40 And ye will not come to me, that ye might have life.

41 I receive not honour from men. 42 But I know you, that ye have not the love of God in you. 43 I am come in my Father's name, and ye receive me not : if another shall come in his own name, him ye will receive.

44 How can ye believe, which receive honour one of another, and seek not the honour that cometh from God only ? 45 Do not think that I will accuse you to the Father ; there is one that accuseth you, even Moses, in whom ye trust. 46 For had ye believed Moses, ye would have believed me : for he wrote of me. 47 But if ye believe not his writings, how shall ye believe my words ?

EXPOSITION

After CHRIST'S WITNESS TO HIMSELF (19–29), He tells us of :—

(ii) OTHER WITNESSES TO HIM (30–47), of which there are five. (a) *The Witness of the Baptist* (32–35). Was he competent ? That depends upon two things, moral uprightness, and accurate knowledge. Had John these ? " *The witness which he beareth of Me is true* " (32, 33 ; cf. ch. i). There were both *light* and *heat* in John's testimony (35) which suggests that testimony may be clear, yet cold. How much warmth is there in your witness ? John was but a local lamp ; Jesus is the universal sun.

(b) *The Witness of Christ's Works* (36). This alone should be enough. Read Matthew xi. 1–6. What Christ has done in the world makes a lot of the criticism of Him look very foolish, and the rejection of Him very sinful. Christ's record is His claim, and it is irresistible.

(c) *The Witness of the Father* (37, 38). Three times, in crises, did the Father bear witness to His Son: at His baptism; when the Greeks came to Him (ch. xii); and at the Transfiguration. Look up and read these passages. The Jews claimed to believe God, yet they refused His Son (38): but rejection of the Son is denial of the Father (1 John ii. 23).

(d) *The Witness of the Scriptures* (39–44). The opening words of verse 39, are a statement, not a command (R.V.). These people, and their successors, have the *record*, yet miss the *revelation*; they have the garden without the flowers; the organ without the music; the body without the soul; the altar without the sacrifice. What is the good of that? What is the use of your " going through the Bible," if the Bible does not go through you?

(e) *The Witness of Moses* (45–47). "*He wrote of Me.*" What shall we say of those who welcome the herald and yet reject the King; who believe the prophecy, and yet deny the fulfilment? How illogical is unbelief!

Thought: KNOW THE TRUTH, AND TELL WHAT YOU KNOW.

ST. JOHN vi. 1-14

Title: A PICNIC ON THE HILLSIDE

1 After these things Jesus went over the sea of Galilee, which is the sea of Tiberias. **2** And a great multitude followed him, because they saw his miracles which he did on them that were diseased. **3** And Jesus went up into a mountain, and there he sat with his disciples. **4** And the passover, a feast of the Jews, was nigh.

5 When Jesus then lifted up his eyes, and saw a great company come unto him, he saith unto Philip, Whence shall we buy bread, that these may eat? **6** And this he said to prove him: for he himself knew what he would do.

7 Philip answered him, Two hundred pennyworth of bread is not sufficient for them, that every one of them may take a little. **8** One of his disciples, Andrew, Simon Peter's brother, saith unto him,

9 There is a lad here, which hath five barley loaves, and two small fishes : but what are they among so many ?

10 And Jesus said, Make the men sit down. Now there was much grass in the place. So the men sat down, in number about five thousand. 11 And Jesus took the loaves ; and when he had given thanks, he distributed to the disciples, and the disciples to them that were set down ; and likewise of the fishes as much as they would.

12 When they were filled, he said unto his disciples, Gather up the fragments that remain, that nothing be lost. 13 Therefore they gathered them together, and filled twelve baskets with the fragments of the five barley loaves, which remained over and above unto them that had eaten. 14 Then those men, when they had seen the miracle that Jesus did, said, This is of a truth that prophet that should come into the world.

EXPOSITION

This event is critical in the ministry of Christ. All the Evangelists record it ; few miracles were wrought after it ; it closed the Lord's public Galilean ministry, and hereafter He devotes Himself mainly to His disciples. In the previous chapter Christ claimed to be the *Source* of life ; here He shows and teaches that He is also the *Sustainer* of it. This crowd was certainly curious, and perhaps careless, but Jesus was compassionate, and that saved, and always saves, the situation.

Difficult circumstances are always revealing ; this one was : it revealed *three* persons, PHILIP, ANDREW, and JESUS. Shall we say *four—the lad* ? Surely. Well, PHILIP calculates, and comes down on the wrong side (7). He looked at the crowd, and then at seven pounds, thirty-five dollars, and concluded that the thing could not be done(5). He had forgotten that his Master had turned water into wine, and, if necessary, could turn stones into bread. Forgetfulness may make an infidel of you.

Enter Andrew (8). He suggests, but doubts, that however, is one better than Philip. Andrew is like a person who goes to bathe, but who, feeling the chilly water, fears to take the plunge. If only some one would push these people in. The world is full of trembling enterprisers, with more of *tremble* then *enterprise*. However, Andrew's suggestion proved fruitful through the generosity of a lad who readily put all that he had into the commissariat (9).

Christ can do much with little, and He would do it through you and me. Remember David and his sling, Shamgar and his ox-goad, Dorcas and her needle. Only Christ could provide for five thousand unexpected guests. Probably the number was nearer fifteen thousand, as the five thousand were men only. Sit down when and where He tells you, and open your mouth wide. There was more at the end of that meal than at the beginning. God is the great Economist, He wastes nothing (12, 13).

Thought : DINE WITH JESUS TO-DAY.

ST. JOHN vi. 15-27
Title : A CHOPPY SEA

15 When Jesus therefore perceived that they would come and take him by force, to make him a king, he departed again into a mountain himself alone.

16 And when even was now come, his disciples went down unto the sea. 17 And entered into a ship, and went over the sea toward Capernaum. And it was now dark, and Jesus was not come to them. 18 And the sea arose by reason of a great wind that blew. 19 So when they had rowed about five and twenty or thirty furlongs, they see Jesus walking on the sea, and drawing nigh unto the ship : and they were afraid. 20 But he saith unto them, It is I ; be not afraid. 21 Then they willingly received him into the ship ; and immediately the ship was at the land whither they went.

22 The day following, when the people which stood on the other side of the sea saw that there was none other boat there, save that one whereinto his disciples were entered, and that Jesus went not with his disciples into the boat, but that his disciples were gone away alone ; 23 (Howbeit there came

other boats from Tiberias nigh unto the place where they did eat bread, after that the Lord had given thanks :)   24 When the people therefore saw that Jesus was not there, neither his disciples, they also took shipping, and came to Capernaum, seeking for Jesus.   25 And when they had found him on the other side of the sea, they said unto him, Rabbi when camest thou hither ?

26 Jesus answered them and said, Verily, verily, I say unto you, Ye seek me, not because ye saw the miracles, but because ye did eat of the loaves, and were filled.   27 Labour not for the meat which perisheth, but for the meat which endureth unto everlasting life, which the Son of man shall give unto you ; for him hath God the Father sealed.

EXPOSITION

Surveying the whole of this chapter we mark three divisions. The subject of the whole is, CHRIST THE BREAD OF LIFE, and it divides up as follows :— *The Illustration* (1–15). *The Interruption* (15–25). *The Interpretation* (26–71).

Throughout this Gospel *incident* is made the occasion of *instruction*, discourse is based on event. The healing of the impotent man led to the discourse on CHRIST'S PERSON AND AUTHORITY (ch. 5) ; here, the feeding of the five thousand leads to the discourse on CHRIST THE BREAD OF LIFE (ch. 6) ; and the healing of the blind man led to the revelation of CHRIST THE LIGHT OF THE WORLD (ch. ix). Trace others.

In our chapter the *Text* (1–14) is separated from the *Sermon* (26–71) by an event on the Sea of Galilee (15–25). It is noteworthy that Jesus resorted to prayer both before and after critical events in His ministry (15). Let us admit at once that we do not pray enough ; we are not enough *alone*. Well, the disciples are sent forward, and run into a storm. Christ has not promised His people a smooth passage, but only a safe landing. In embarking upon the Christian life we are not guaranteed a sun-lit sea ; rather are we advised of a storm-tossed ocean, *but we are promised the presence of Christ*; and it is far better to be in a storm with Him, than in a calm without Him.

The trouble is that too often we do not recognise Him when He comes (19). It is good for us to have the discipline of the storm, but this means of grace becomes an occasion of disaster if we doubt the faithfulness and power of Christ. Let us learn also, that we are not to be inactive in our storms ; Christ comes to the aid of the honest rower (19).

How pathetic is this wandering crowd of which we have read (22–27), and how patient is the Master. These people loved Jesus for His bread, and therefore loved the bread more than Jesus. Mark the double paradox in verse 27. The people are told that they should not labour for the perishable food, which is the very thing they must get by working ; and that they should labour for the heavenly food, which is not to be earned by labour.

Thought : *SEEK CHRIST FOR HIMSELF ALONE* (26).

ST. JOHN vi. 28-40

Title : *THE BREAD OF LIFE*

28 Then said they unto him, What shall we do that we might work the works of God ?

29 Jesus answered and said unto them, This is the work of God, that ye believe on him whom he hath sent.

30 They said therefore unto him, What sign shewest thou then, that we may see, and believe thee ? what dost thou work ? 31 Our fathers did eat manna in the desert ; as it is written, He gave them bread from heaven to eat.

32 Then Jesus said unto them, Verily, verily, I say unto you, Moses gave you not that bread from heaven ; but my Father giveth you the true bread from heaven. 33 For the bread of God is he which cometh down from heaven, and giveth life unto the world.

34 Then said they unto him, Lord, evermore give us this bread.

35 And Jesus said unto them, I am the bread of life : he that cometh to me shall never hunger ; and he that believeth on me shall never thirst. 36 But I said unto you, That ye also have seen me, and believe not. 37 All that the Father giveth me shall come to me ; and him that cometh to me I will in no wise cast out. 38 For I came down from heaven, not to do mine own will, but the will of him that sent me. 39 And this is the Father's will which hath sent me, that of all which he hath given me I should lose nothing, but should raise it up again at the last day. 40 And this is the will of him that sent me, that every one which seeth the Son, and believeth on him, may have everlasting life : and I will raise him up at the last day.

EXPOSITION

Our Lord's discourse is in two parts. In part one (26-40). He addresses the *Crowd* : and in part two (41-59), the *Jews*. Verses 26, 27, expound the text, " man shall not live by bread *alone.*" He must have bread, but he should have more : we need victuals, but we need vision also. If man were only body, bread would be enough ; but as he is also soul, he needs God as well. All through the ages men have been asking what they must do to inherit eternal life (28), and the answer every time has been— *believe on Jesus Christ* (29).

When that point is reached, people generally attempt to evade it (30). These people suggested that there was not enough evidence to call forth faith. What about the meal they had had on the hillside ? How much evidence are you demanding in order to find Christ trustworthy ? The fact is, evidence is heaped heaven-high ; what we need is eyes to see it, and a heart to desire it. Pray for that.

The people were hungry (34) ; everybody is. The undertones of the world tell of universal spiritual hunger ; yet there is " *bread enough and to spare.*" However, it is not to be found in the " far off country," but in the Father's house. The great truth of this part of the discourse is, that CHRIST IS THE BREAD

OF LIFE, and THE WATER OF LIFE (35). Then say to Him just now :—

> "Thou bruised and broken Bread,
> My life-long wants supply ;
> As living souls are fed,
> O, feed me, or I die."

The sight of bread will feed no one ; it must be eaten (36). At this hour there are people perishing because they are more intent upon analysing the loaf than they are eager to eat it. "*Him that cometh unto Me I will in no wise cast out.*" Turn that sweet morsel over in your mouth.

And further, Jesus says, not only that He can *satisfy*, but also that He will *glorify* (39, 40). If you will have Him *every day*, you shall have Him *at the last day*.

Thought : *IF TO-DAY YOU DO NOT WANT WHAT YOU NEED, SOME DAY YOU WILL NEED WHAT YOU WANT.*

ST. JOHN vi. 41-59

Title : *SIMPLE FARE*

41 The Jews then murmured at him, because he said, I am the bread which came down from heaven. **42** And they said, Is not this Jesus, the son of Joseph, whose father and mother we know ? how is it then that he saith, I came down from heaven ?

43 Jesus therefore answered and said unto them, Murmur not among yourselves. **44** No man can come to me, except the Father which hath sent me draw him : and I will raise him up at the last day. **45** It is written in the prophets, And they shall be all taught of God. Every man therefore that hath heard, and hath learned of the Father, cometh unto me. **46** Not that any man hath seen the Father, save he which is of God, he hath seen the Father.

47 Verily, verily, I say unto you, He that believeth on me hath everlasting life. **48** I am that bread of life. **49** Your fathers did eat manna in the wilderness, and are dead. **50** This is the bread which cometh down from heaven, that a man may eat thereof, and not die. **51 I am the living bread which came down from heaven : if any man eat of this bread, he shall live for ever : and the bread that I will give is my flesh, which I will give for the life of the world.**

52 The Jews therefore strove among themselves, saying, How can this man give us his flesh to eat ?

53 Then Jesus said unto them, Verily, verily, I say unto you, Except ye eat the flesh of the Son of man, and drink his blood, ye have no life in you. 54 Whoso eateth my flesh, and drinketh my blood, hath eternal life : and I will raise him up at the last day. 55 For my flesh is meat indeed, and my blood is drink indeed. 56 He that eateth my flesh, and drinketh my blood, dwelleth in me, and I in him. 57 As the living Father hath sent me, and I live by the Father : so he that eateth me, even he shall live by me. 58 This is that bread which came down from heaven : not as your fathers did eat manna, and are dead : he that eateth of this bread shall live for ever.

59 These things said he in the synagogue, as he taught in Capernaum.

EXPOSITION

Let us keep in mind the main outline of this longest chapter in a book of long chapters : In verses 1–15, is Illustration ; in 16–25 is Interruption ; and in 26–71 is Interpretation (of verses 1–15). The first part of our Lord's discourse is to the *crowd* (26–40), and the second part is to the *Jews* (41–59).

There is nothing so profound as simplicity. Every one understands the meaning of " bread and water." yet, who can fathom the meaning of our Lord's words ! The Jews took them literally (52) and so do sacredotalists ; but their value is wholly spiritual. Leaving the simplicity of Christ we have elaborated theological sciences and intricate creeds. We have worked out cunning symbolisms ; we have filled the church with incense, with garments of many colours and with many significances. We have called Councils and Synods and Congresses. We have constituted a splendid hierarchy with mitres and crooks, and clothing with precious gold and glaring with ardent colouring. We have formed long processions of reverends, most reverends, right reverends, and very reverends; doctors and deans and eminences and holinesses—yet Jesus called Himself "*Bread and Water.*"

He came from the Father, went to the Father, and alone interprets the Father. We do not know Jesus by knowing God, but we know God by knowing Jesus. The manna in the wilderness was typical. Christ is the reality of which that was the symbol. The trouble is that people stumble at the manner of the Divine manifestation (42). God revealed and reveals Himself in ways familiar to us and understandable. The *incarnation*, together with its purpose, is the key alike to history and philosophy. Have you eaten that *Bread* and drunk of that *Water*? Discussing them will not save, but appropriation and assimilation will.

Thought: "*EAT, O FRIENDS, DRINK, YEA, DRINK ABUNDANTLY, O BELOVED*" (*Cant.* v. 1).

ST. JOHN vi. 60-71

Title: DIVERSE RESULTS

60 Many therefore of his disciples, when they had heard this, said, This is an hard saying; who can bear it?
61 When Jesus knew in himself that his disciples murmured at it, he said unto them, Doth this offend you? 62 What and if ye shall see the Son of man ascend up where he was before? 63 It is the spirit that quickeneth; the flesh profiteth nothing: the words that I speak unto you, they are spirit, and they are life. 64 But there are some of you that believe not. For Jesus knew from the beginning who they were that believed not, and who should betray him. 65 And he said, Therefore said I unto you, that no man can come unto me, except it were given unto him of my Father.

66 From that time many of his disciples went back, and walked no more with him.

67 Then said Jesus unto the twelve, Will ye also go away?

68 Then Simon Peter answered him, Lord, to whom shall we go? thou hast the words of eternal life. 69 And we believe and are sure that thou art that Christ, the Son of the living God.

70 Jesus answered them, Have not I chosen you twelve, and one of you is a devil? 71 He spake of Judas Iscariot the son of Simon: for he it was that should betray him, being one of the twelve.

EXPOSITION

The remainder of this chapter is occupied with THE EFFECTS OF JESUS' DISCOURSE, first, *upon professed disciples* (60–66), and then, *upon the chosen Twelve* (67–71). Look at the first of these.

The Master never trimmed His message to keep the crowd: would that His followers had never done so. When He saw that some who professed to be His disciples (60–66) stumbled at His teaching (61) He just repeated and re-emphasised it (62, 63), because, He knew that the real difficulty was not intellectual but spiritual (64). The final rejection of Christ is never due to want of *mind*, but to want of *faith*. Make a note of that.

Christ wants true friends, not a loosely attached crowd. There are always people who are true only as long as the trough is full; who are ready to cancel all the obligations of the past on account of a difficulty in the present. The strength of a church is not in the length of its Members' Roll. I know of a church which had a revival after some people had left it.

Now look at the effect of this Discourse upon the Twelve (67–71). Jesus was prepared to be left alone. When He saw the people melting away, He asked the Twelve if they were going too. He does not want to do without you and me, but He *can*. It is to our advantage to have Him, not to His to have us. You are not doing God a favour by accepting the Gospel; He is doing you a favour by offering it.

Well, if we who profess to be Christ's disciples leave Him, to whom shall we go ? We must always take into account the alternatives. Compare this great confession of Peter's (68, 69) with that other in Matthew xvi. Peter rose on occasions to great heights of faith. He here says, " *we believe and are sure.*" In that word faith and reason blend. Devotion should never be the child of ignorance. Peter's confession is a great creed. Only those who believe are Believers ; only followers of Christ are Christians ; only those who are pure are Puritans. What a mystery *Judas* was and is (70, 71) !

Thought : *CHRIST'S NEED IS OUR OPPORTUNITY.*

ST. JOHN vii. 1-18

Title : *APPROACHING DANGER*

1 After these things Jesus walked in Galilee : for he would not walk in Jewry, because the Jews sought to kill him. 2 Now the Jews' feast of tabernacles was at hand. 3 His brethren therefore said unto him, Depart hence, and go into Judæa, that thy disciples also may see the works that thou doest. 4 For there is no man that doeth any thing in secret, and he himself seeketh to be known openly. If thou do these things, shew thyself to the world. 5 For neither did his brethren believe in him.

6 Then Jesus said unto them, My time is not yet come : but your time is alway ready. 7 The world cannot hate you : but me it hateth, because I testify of it, that the works thereof are evil. 8 Go ye up unto this feast ; I go not up yet unto this feast : for my time is not yet full come.

9 When he had said these words unto them, he abode still in Galilee.

10 But when his brethren were gone up, then went he also up unto the feast, not openly, but as it were in secret.

11 Then the Jews sought him at the feast, and said, Where is he ? 12 And there was much murmuring among the people concerning him : for some said, He is a good man : others said, Nay ;

but he deceiveth the people. 13 Howbeit no man spake openly of him for fear of the Jews.

14 Now about the midst of the feast Jesus went up into the temple, and taught. 15 And the Jews marvelled, saying, How knowest this man letters, having never learned ?

16 Jesus answered them, and said, My doctrine is not mine, but his that sent me. 17 If any man will do his will, he shall know of the doctrine, whether it be of God, or whether I speak of myself. 18 He that speaketh of himself seeketh his own glory : but he that seeketh his glory that sent him, the same is true, and no unrighteousness is in him.

EXPOSITION

Let us stop a moment to get again the perspective of this Record. THE LIFE ANNOUNCED (i. 19 to ii. 22), and ACKNOWLEDGED (ii. 23 to iv. 54), is ANTAGONISED (v to xii) ; and in this last division the Controversy is first *Aroused* (v. 1-18), then *Developed* (v. 19, to x), and then *Concluded* (xi and xii). Under the section, *The Controversy Developed*, we see THE LIFE DESPISED (v, vi) ; THE LIGHT REFUSED (vii-ix) ; and THE LOVE OUTRAGED (x).

Now, you can easily see where our present portion falls. In chapter vi, the teaching follows the miracle, but here it precedes it, the teaching on Light being given in chaps. vii, viii, and the illustration following in chap. ix. Between chaps. vi. and vii, a period of seven months has elapsed, and from now on Jesus is devoting Himself mainly to His disciples.

It may be said that in chaps. i.-vi. we see mainly the development of *belief*, but in chaps. vii.-xii. of *unbelief*. Our chapter is in three parts circling round the *Feast of Tabernacles* : 1-13, Before the Feast ; 14-36, During the Feast ; 37-52, End of the Feast.

1. BEFORE THE FEAST (1-13). Observe here *why Jesus could not continue to teach in Judea* (1) ; *the attitude of His brothers towards Him* (2-10) ; and *the diverse opinions concerning Him among the people at Jerusalem* (11-13). It is a sad and tragic fact that

some who were nearest the light were most blind (5). Have you unsaved brothers and sisters who make it difficult for you at home ? Then, for your comfort, remember that Jesus also had such. The Master's life was directed by the will of the Father, and He here speaks of a divinity of chronology (6–8). God never is before His time, and never is behind. Sometimes we err in being too quick, and sometimes in being too slow. There is an hour for everything.

Christ has always been a problem (12) ; opinion has always been divided about Him. One of the dominating questions in every generation is, *What think ye of Christ ?* The " *Good* " will not " *deceive*," and deceivers are not good.

Thought : JESUS HAD A HARD TIME AT HOME.

ST. JOHN vii. 19-36

Title : FACING OPPOSITION

19 Did not Moses give you the law, and yet none of you keepeth the law ? Why go ye about to kill me ?

20 The people answered and said, Thou hast a devil : who goeth about to kill thee ?

21 Jesus answered and said unto them, I have done one work, and ye all marvel. **22** Moses therefore gave unto you circumcision ; (not because it is of Moses, but of the fathers ;) and ye on the sabbath day circumcise a man. **23** If a man on the sabbath day receive circumcision, that the law of Moses should not be broken ; are ye angry at me, because I have made a man every whit whole on the sabbath day ? **24** Judge not according to the appearance, but judge righteous judgment.

25 Then said some of them of Jerusalem, Is not this he, whom they seek to kill ? **26** But, lo, he speaketh boldly, and they say nothing unto him. Do the rulers know indeed that this is the very Christ ? **27** Howbeit we know this man whence he is : but when Christ cometh, no man knoweth whence he is.

28 Then cried Jesus in the temple as he taught,

saying, Ye both know me, and ye know whence I am : and I am not come of myself, but he that sent me is true, whom ye know not. 29 But I know him : for I am from him, and he hath sent me.

30 Then they sought to take him ; but no man laid hands on him, because his hour was not yet come. 31 And many of the people believed on him, and said, When Christ cometh, will he do more miracles than these which this man hath done ?

32 The Pharisees heard that the people murmured such things concerning him ; and the Pharisees and the chief priests sent officials to take him.

33 Then said Jesus unto them, Yet a little while am I with you, and then I go unto him that sent me. 34 Ye shall seek me, and shall not find me : and where I am, thither ye cannot come.

35 Then said the Jews among themselves, Whither will he go, that we shall not find him ? will he go unto the dispersed among the Gentiles, and teach the Gentiles ? 36 What manner of saying is this that he said, Ye shall seek me, and shall not find me : and where I am, thither ye cannot come ?

EXPOSITION

2. DURING THE FEAST (14–36). The presence of Christ is always revealing ; He brings to light the secret things, and lays open the hidden thoughts of men. This is true not of one class only, but of all. Here, there are three distinct cycles of discussion.

(i) *With the Jews* (14–24). Is it not true that certain ideas are well-nigh immortal—wrong ideas, I mean. Here is one of them, that in order to be accredited you must graduate at one or other of the Schools (15). Well, that would have disqualified both Spurgeon and Moody, and long before them, both Peter and John, and their Master. I am all for all the culture we can get, but for culture-snobbery I have a deep-seated contempt.

Another lesson here is, you can test the truth by trying it (17). Christianity is not a controversy, but a character which expresses itself in conduct. These Jews claimed kinship with Moses, but Moses would not have owned one of them. " Natural relations are forfeited by moral apostasy." They only have a right to claim Abraham, and Moses, and Christ, who are of their spirit. In verses 21-23, we have an echo of chapter v.

(ii) *With the People* (25-31). Here again the person of Jesus is the focus of controversy. Who is He ? It is pathetic when people announcing their knowledge only advertise their ignorance (27). They remembered Nazareth, but forgot Bethlehem. What you are *forgetting* may rob you of Christ. Jesus' answer brought light and life to some (31), while it stirred up hatred in others (30). The former caught the vision, but the latter caught the voltage.

(iii) *With the Envoys* (32-36). When they came to Him, it was only to learn that He was going from them (33, 34). If to-day the seeking Saviour is neglected, to-morrow the seeking sinner will be rejected. They who would find Him must be found of Him. These messengers were deeply impressed by what Jesus said to them (46). What effect have preaching and teaching upon you ?

Thought : *THE TRUTH IS ALWAYS EQUAL TO THE STORM.*

ST. JOHN vii. 37-53

Title : *THE FOUNTAIN AND THE RIVER*

37 In the last day, that great day of the feast, Jesus stood and cried, saying, If any thirst, let him come unto me, and drink. 38 He that believeth on me, as the scripture hath said, out of his belly shall flow rivers of living water. 39 (But this spake he of the Spirit, which they that believe on him should receive ; for the Holy Ghost was not yet given ; because that Jesus was not yet glorified).

40 Many of the people therefore, when they heard this saying, said, Of a truth this is the Prophet. 41 Others said, This is the Christ. But some said, Shall Christ come out of Galilee ? 42 Hath not the scripture said, That Christ cometh of the seed of David, and out of the town of Bethlehem

where David was? 43 So there was a division among the people because of him. 44 And some of them would have taken him ; but no man laid hands on him.

45 Then came the officers to the chief priests and Pharisees : and they said unto them, Why have ye not brought him ? 46 The officers answered, Never man spake like this man. 47 Then answered them the Pharisees, Are ye also deceived ? 48 Have any of the rulers or of the Pharisees believed on him ? 49 But this people who knoweth not the law are cursed.

50 Nicodemus saith unto them, (he that came to Jesus by night, being one of them,) 51 Doth our law judge any man, before it hear him, and know what he doeth ? 52 They answered and said unto him, Art thou also of Galilee ? Search, and look : for out of Galilee ariseth no prophet. 53 And every man went unto his own house.

EXPOSITION

See the two preceding portions for the connection.

3. END OF THE FEAST (37–52). The last day was the greatest. Alike the courage and grace of Christ are sublime ; *courage*, in the " loud cry " of verse 28 ; and *grace* in His " loud cry " here (37). When He speaks of " *thirst* " He tells of need ; when of " *drink* " He tells of supply ; and when He says " *come* " He shows how alone the need and the supply can be brought together. The Fountain is ever flowing : are you ever thirsting ? Remember, if you do not drink you rob not only yourself but other people also (38). Of him who is ever drinking it is said that out of his vitals there shall ever be flowing " *rivers* of *living water.*" Are you a river, or a dry rut ? Before there can be the outflow there must be the inflow.

The Evangelist, sixty years after this utterance, explains it, and does so in the light of history and experience (39). Not until Jesus was glorified historically, was the Spirit given, and not until He is glorified spiritually in your heart and life, do you know His Spirit. Then *Come, Drink, Flow*. This sublime utterance of our Lord's set all the people guessing (40–44). Is He the Prophet? Or the Christ? Or neither? No one can really know who Christ is until he trusts Him: some things can be known only from the inside. It is not a matter of geography and chronology (42), but of repentance and faith. Christ was like an electric current, scattering to right and left all the diverse elements through which it passes.

Now enter the officers again (45, 32), but without Jesus. His *words* had conquered their *weapons* (46); His majesty had paralysed their might. Nicodemus comes again into view, the night school pupil (50–52). He got only abuse for his loyalty to principle, but it is only the weak and the mean who fall back upon abuse. Are you strong enough to stand alone for Jesus?

Thought: *LISTEN TO THE WORLD'S GREATEST SPEAKER* (46).

ST. JOHN viii. 1-11

Title: *ALL SINNERS BUT ONE*

1 Jesus went unto the mount of Olives.
2 And early in the morning he came again into the temple, and all the people came unto him; and he sat down, and taught them.
3 And the scribes and Pharisees brought unto him a woman taken in adultery; and when they had set her in the midst, 4 They say unto him, Master, this woman was taken in adultery, in the very act. 5 Now Moses in the law commanded us, that such should be stoned: but what sayest thou? 6 This they said, tempting him, that they might have to accuse him.

But Jesus stooped down, and with his finger wrote on the ground, as though he heard them not. **7 So when they continued asking him, he lifted up himself, and said unto them, He that is without sin among you, let him first cast a stone at her. 8 And again he stooped down, and wrote on the ground.**

9 And they which heard it, being convicted by

their own conscience, went out one by one, beginning at the eldest, even unto the last: and Jesus was left alone, and the woman standing in the midst. 10 When Jesus had lifted up himself, and saw none but the woman, he said unto her, Woman, where are those thine accusers? hath no man condemned thee? 11 She said, No man, Lord. And Jesus said unto her, Neither do I condemn thee: go, and sin no more.

EXPOSITION

" This account," says Westcott, " of a most characteristic incident in the Lord's life is certainly not a part of St. John's narrative. The evidence against its genuineness, as an original piece of the Gospel, both external and internal, is overwhelming; but on the other hand it is beyond doubt an authentic fragment of apostolic tradition. Probably its preservation was due to Papias. The incident seems to belong to the last visit to Jerusalem; and it is placed in this connection in some MSS. of St. Luke (after Luke xxi)."

Verse 53 of the previous chapter belongs to the beginning of this chapter. Jesus found it necessary often to be alone (1). Do you? It is ruinous to spend all of our time in company, however good; we need to be much alone with God.

Jesus frequented the Temple and Synagogues, or, as we would say, He went to Church (2). They who do not, miss much. I am not referring to the sermon, sometimes that is pretty bad, but to Church as a meeting place for public worship. But all who go to Church do not go to worship. These men did not (3). They went there to lay a snare for the Saviour. Their unholy souls went to the Holy Place. They were keener on exposing the sins of others than of confessing their own. They called Jesus *"Teacher,"* but they did not come to be taught (4). They professed reverence for the Mosaic Law, but they were, by the act in which they were engaged, violating the spirit of that Law (5, 6).

This is the only time we hear of Christ *writing* (6),

and then He *wrote on the ground*. "*O, earth, earth, earth, hear the word of the Lord*" (Jer. xxii. 29). I wonder what He wrote! His action indicates an unwillingness to answer the question which was put to Him. But, as the inquirers are insistent, they shall have an answer (7). "*Let the sinless man among you be the first to throw a stone at her.*"

Jesus is not charging each of them with the sin of adultery, but with the sinful inclination which had, in this woman's case, issued in the sinful act. Freedom from outward guilt does not carry with it freedom from inward sin, and the outward guilt does not cut one off from hope. These men were made to feel the one truth (7–9), and the woman, the other (10, 11). When Christ said that He did not *condemn* the woman, He did not mean that He *condoned* her sin. His word to us all is, "*sin no more.*"

Thought: "*HIS BLOOD CAN MAKE THE VILEST CLEAN.*"

ST. JOHN viii. 12-30

Title: *CHRIST IS GOD MANIFEST IN THE FLESH*

12 Then spake Jesus again unto them, saying, I am the light of the world : he that followeth me shall not walk in darkness, but shall have the light of life.
13 The Pharisees therefore said unto him, Thou bearest record of thyself ; thy record is not true.
14 Jesus answered and said unto them, Though I bear record of myself, yet my record is true : for I know whence I came, and whither I go ; but ye cannot tell whence I come, and whither I go. **15** Ye judge after the flesh ; I judge no man. **16** And yet if I judge, my judgment is true : for I am not alone, but I and the Father that sent me. **17** It is also written in your law, that the testimony of two men is true. **18** I am one that bear witness of myself, and the Father that sent me beareth witness of me.

19 Then said they unto him, Where is thy Father? Jesus answered, Ye neither know me, nor my Father: if ye had known me, ye should have known my Father also.

20 These words spake Jesus in the treasury, as he taught in the temple: and no man laid hands on him; for his hour was not yet come.

21 Then said Jesus again unto them, I go my way, and ye shall seek me, and shall die in your sins: whither I go, ye cannot come.

22 Then said the Jews, Will he kill himself? because he saith, Whither I go, ye cannot come.

23 And he said unto them, Ye are from beneath; I am from above: ye are of this world; I am not of this world. 24 I said therefore unto you, that ye shall die in your sins: for if ye believe not that I am he, ye shall die in your sins.

25 Then said they unto him, Who art thou?

And Jesus saith unto them, Even the same that I said unto you from the beginning. 26 I have many things to say and to judge of you: but he that sent me is true; and I speak to the world those things which I have heard of him.

27 They understood not that he spake to them of the Father.

28 Then said Jesus unto them, When ye have lifted up the Son of man, then shall ye know that I am he, and that I do nothing of myself; but as my Father hath taught me, I speak these things. 29 And he that sent me is with me: the Father hath not left me alone; for I do always those things that please him.

30 As he spake these words, many believed on him.

EXPOSITION

In verses 12–20 Jesus bears a *witness*; and in 21–30, He issues a *warning*. The Master had already likened Himself to the *riven rock* (vii. 37); now He claims to be the true *fiery pillar* directing and regulating the march of His people through the wilderness. The Jews did not believe His testimony, because, they said, it was unsupported. But Jesus affirmed that it was *not* unsupported, for His Father also bore witness of Him (18).

Utterly ignorant of Who He was Who was speaking to them, they thought only of an earthly father (19) ; but in an utterance of penetrating lucidity and power Jesus declares that He was the revelation of His Father, and that, for lack of sympathy, the Jews knew neither of them. Let us remember that *sympathy is always needed in order to understanding.*

From this *witness*, Jesus passes on to a solemn *warning* (21-30), in which He presents the one true object of faith, and declares what are the consequences of unbelief. Mark here the thrice repeated " *ye shall die in your sins.*" How unspeakably terrible a possibility. "To die without Christ, hast thou counted the cost ? " Mark also the thrice repeated " *I am* " (24, 28, 58), which is one of the keys of this Gospel. Trace through its pages what Christ claimed to be ; " *I am the Light,*" " *I am the Bread of life,*" " *I am the Door,*" and others.

The Truth insisted on in this discourse is that unbelief and death go together, as do faith and life. The Son's perfect oneness with the Father is made evident by the habit of His life, and quality of His service (29). His was not a negative obedience merely, a cold abstinence from evil, but a service at once positive, active, and energetic. We can have no greater ambition in life than to be *well-pleasing in His sight.* Underline Christ's references in this chapter to His FATHER.

Thought : THEY WHO HEAR THE TRUTH SHOULD TRUST HIM.

ST. JOHN viii. 31-47

Title : NATURAL AND MORAL PEDIGREES

31 Then said Jesus to those Jews which believed on him, If ye continue in my word, then are ye my disciples indeed ; 32 And ye shall know the truth, and the truth shall make you free.

33 They answered him, We be Abraham's seed, and were never in bondage to any man : how sayest thou, Ye shall be made free ?

34 Jesus answered them, Verily, verily, I say unto you, Whosoever committeth sin is the servant of sin. **35** And the servant abideth not in the house for ever: but the Son abideth ever. **36** If the Son therefore shall make you free, ye shall be free indeed. **37** I know that ye are Abraham's seed; but ye seek to kill me, because my word hath no place in you. **38** I speak that which I have seen with my Father: and ye do that which ye have seen with your father.

39 They answered and said unto him, Abraham is our father. Jesus saith unto them, If ye were Abraham's children, ye would do the works of Abraham. **40** But now ye seek to kill me, a man that hath told you the truth, which I have heard of God: this did not Abraham. **41** Ye do the deeds of your father.

Then said they to him, We be not born of fornication; we have one Father, even God.

42 Jesus said unto them, If God were your Father, ye would love me: for I proceeded forth and came from God: neither came I of myself, but he sent me. **43** Why do ye not understand my speech? even because ye cannot hear my word. **44** Ye are of your father the devil, and the lusts of your father ye will do. He was a murderer from the beginning, and abode not in the truth, because there is no truth in him. When he speaketh a lie, he speaketh of his own: for he is a liar, and the father of it. **45** And because I tell you the truth, ye believe me not.

46 Which of you convinceth me of sin? And if I say the truth, why do ye not believe me? **47** He that is of God heareth God's words: ye therefore hear them not, because ye are not of God.

EXPOSITION

Had verse 30 ended the interview between Jesus and these Jews, how different would have been the impression left upon us, and how different the remainder of the story. But alas, the faith of these people was a mirage and not a pool, as what follows plainly shows.

Christ promises FREEDOM to those who honestly follow out an imperfect faith (31, 32). Mark in these verses *a cause*, continuance; *a means*, knowledge; and *an end*, freedom. But the Jews claimed never to have been in bondage; whereupon Jesus makes a great declaration which is true always, everywhere, that "*whoso committeth sin is the servant of sin.*" We sing, "Britons never, never shall be slaves," but are not numberless Britons slaves? bound by the chains of greed, indulgence, selfishness, pride, lust, and much beside? Sin is always enslaving, so that *if you are a sinner you are a slave*. Do you believe that? No one is the master of sin. Only Christ can make us freemen (36). Has He snapped your chains?

The next word is on PEDIGREE (37-47); and here Jesus declares that natural descent does not carry with it spiritual likeness. Physical and moral kinship and likeness do not always go together. We Gentiles cannot claim natural descent from Abraham, but Paul teaches that "if we be Christ's, then are we Abraham's seed, and heirs according to the promise" (Gal. iii. 29). This truth is definitely applied to the Jews in verses 43-47, where He Who knew, plainly tells them that their father is not God, but the devil. Some people make a great boast of their pedigree, ignorant or forgetful of the fact that *character settles the question of kinship*. According to soul-image whose child are you?

Trace in this Gospel Christ's claims for Himself. Here He claims to be sinless (46). It would be the worst of sins for any one else to make such a claim. Christ never sought pardon, because He never needed it. If you have not sought it, you need pardon for not seeking it.

Thought: *LORD, MAKE ME MORE LIKE THEE TO-DAY.*

ST. JOHN viii. 48-59

Title: *SLANDER AND STONES*

48 Then answered the Jews, and said unto him, Say we not well that thou art a Samaritan, and hast a devil?

49 Jesus answered, I have not a devil; but I honour my Father, and ye do dishonour me. 50 And I seek not mine own glory : there is one that seeketh and judgeth. 51 Verily, verily, I say unto you, If a man keep my saying, he shall never see death.

52 Then said the Jews unto him, Now we know that thou hast a devil. Abraham is dead, and the prophets ; and thou sayest, If a man keep my saying, he shall never taste of death. 53 Art thou greater than our father Abraham, which is dead ? and the prophets are dead : whom makest thou thyself ?

54 Jesus answered, If I honour myself, my honour is nothing : it is my Father that honoureth me ; of whom ye say, that he is your God : 55 Yet ye have not known him ; but I know him : and if I should say, I know him not, I shall be a liar like unto you : but I know him, and keep his saying. 56 Your father Abraham rejoiced to see my day : and he saw it, and was glad.

57 Then said the Jews unto him, Thou art not yet fifty years old, and hast thou seen Abraham ?

58 Jesus said unto them, Verily, verily, I say unto you, Before Abraham was, I am.

59 Then took they up stones to cast at him : but Jesus hid himself, and went out of the temple, going through the midst of them, and so passed by.

EXPOSITION

There are three small paragraphs here, each beginning with something that the Jews said about Jesus.

In the first (48–51) they deliberately and wickedly insult Him by calling Him a Samaritan, though they knew He was a Galilean, and by affirming that He was demon-possessed. Have we any sense of horror when we read these words ? Remember Who He was to Whom they were speaking, and what He had the power to do ; yet He quietly replies, " *Ye do dishonour Me.*" How do you react when you are insulted ?

In the second paragraph (52–56) the Jews take up Jesus' last statement (51), and with a note of absolute certainty reaffirm that He was demon-possessed. All through this controversy Christ and these men are on entirely different levels of thought, although employing the same words. When Jesus spoke about *freedom* (32) they misunderstood Him, as they do now when He speaks of *death*. Christ was a great enigma to them all (25, 53), as in all ages He has been to all who have failed to trust Him. He here plainly answers that He *is* greater than Abraham, known and honoured of God, and knowing Him as they never did or could.

The claims of Christ throughout this debate are astounding, and credible only on the ground that He was more than man, that He was truly God. Underline these claims in your Bible.

In the last paragraph (57-59) the Jews not only entirely misunderstand what Christ has said, but misquote Him. But their sinful hate and unreasoned rage draw from the Master another mighty claim, and one which led these men to murderous action, " BEFORE ABRAHAM WAS, I AM." The Greek reads, " before Abraham was born, I AM." " Was " implies *creation*, but " am " implies *existence*. Jesus is the Jehovah of the Old Testament. By this title He claims to be God (Exod. iii. 14). Let us remember that He Who WAS, and WILL BE, always IS.

Imagine! Casting stones at the Sovereign of the Universe! Worship at His feet just now.

Thought: THINK OF THE MORAL MAJESTY OF CHRIST.

ST. JOHN ix. 1-12

Title: LIGHT FOR DARKNESS

1 And as Jesus passed by, he saw a man which was blind from his birth. 2 And his disciples asked him, saying, Master, who did sin, this man, or his parents, that he was born blind?

3 Jesus answered, Neither hath this man sinned, nor his parents but that the works of God should be made manifest in him. 4 I must work the works of him that sent me, while it is day: the night

cometh, when no man can work. 5 As long as I am in the world, I am the light of the world.

6 When he had thus spoken, he spat on the ground, and made clay of the spittle, and he anointed the eyes of the blind man with the clay. 7 And said unto him, Go, wash in the pool of Siloam, (which is by interpretation, Sent). He went his way therefore, and washed, and came seeing.

8 The neighbours therefore, and they which before had seen him that he was blind, said, Is not this he that sat and begged? 9 Some said, This is he : other said, He is like him : but he said, I am he.

10 Therefore said they unto him, How were thine eyes opened? 11 He answered and said, A man that is called Jesus made clay, and anointed mine eyes, and said unto me, Go to the pool of Siloam, and wash : and I went and washed, and I received sight.

12 Then said they unto him, Where is he? He said, I know not.

EXPOSITION

Make a note in the margin of your Bible now of the main divisions of this graphic story. There are seven : BENEFACTION (1–7), CONSTERNATION (8, 9), EXAMINATION (10–23), CONFESSION (24–33), PERSECUTION (34), REVELATION (35–38), CONDEMNATION 39–x. 21). Let us now think about these.

1. THE BENEFACTION (1–7). Jesus opens the eyes of a man who had been born blind. He is still *passing by* (1), and He sees *you*, sees you as you *are*, and as you *should be*. He is not out as a sight-seer, but as a sight-giver. *Born blind !* What a calamity ! Yet spiritually this is the state of us all by nature (Eph. v. 8) : but the Light of the world stands in the midst. The disciples made two mistakes (2) : first, they attributed specific suffering to specific sin. That was the mistake of Job's " friends," and of many since their time. Of course it may be so, but it is not necessarily so ; it was not so in this case.

The second mistake was that instead of being moved to pity by the sight of this man, they proposed a theological discussion, a philosophical puzzle. How often we *talk* when we should *help*. Jesus said, " *I must work* " (4). He did not come into the world to explain evil, but to triumph over it. The day of our opportunity is very limited ; therefore, let us *work*. We can help the world only as long as we are in it (5). Jesus, adopting means, gives this man sight (6, 7), and great is—

2. THE CONSTERNATION (8, 9) which follows. " Is not this he ? " " This is he." " He is like him." " I am he." The thing is full of humour. The converted ought always to arouse curiosity. If your profession of Christ has not changed you, you have good ground for misgiving. Study carefully the questions and answers in—

3. THE EXAMINATION. *The neighbours* (10–12). How ? Where ? How direct and simple are the replies. It is experience that gives power to testimony.

Thought : BE BUSY TILL YOUR SUN SETS (4).

ST. JOHN ix. 13-25

Title : A CONTROVERSY OVER CHRIST

13 They brought to the Pharisees him that aforetime was blind. 14 And it was the sabbath day when Jesus made the clay, and opened his eyes.

15 Then again the Pharisees also asked him how he had received his sight.

He said unto them, He put clay upon mine eyes, and I washed, and do see.

16 Therefore said some of the Pharisees, This man is not of God, because he keepeth not the sabbath day. Others said, How can a man that is a sinner do such miracles ? And there was a division among them.

17 They say unto the blind man again, What sayest thou of him, that he hath opened thine eyes ?

He said, He is a prophet.

18 But the Jews did not believe concerning him, that he had been blind, and received his sight, until they called the parents of him that had received his sight. 19 And they asked them, saying, Is this

your son, who ye say was born blind? how then doth he now see?

20 His parents answered and said, We know that this is our son, and that he was born blind: 21 But by what means he now seeth, we know not; or who hath opened his eyes, we know not: he is of age; ask him: he shall speak for himself. 22 These words spake his parents, because they feared the Jews: for the Jews had agreed already, that if any man did confess that he was Christ, he should be put out of the synagogue. 23 Therefore said his parents, He is of age; ask him.

24 Then again called they the man that was blind, and said unto him, Give God the praise: we know that this man is a sinner.

25 He answered and said, Whether he be a sinner or no, I know not: one thing I know, that, whereas I was blind, now I see.

EXPOSITION

Glance at the preceding portion again and follow still.

3. THE EXAMINATION of this man. He is cross-examined first by his neighbours, and then by the Pharisees: his parents also are questioned. What a comedy this is! The contemptibleness of the Pharisees, the cowardice of the parents, and the courage of the man himself, all give vivid colour to the picture. The first objection of the Pharisees is, that the man was healed *on the Sabbath day*. Well, is there a better day in the week on which to do good? Surely all that Jesus has ever done on a Sabbath day has been worthy of the day; but many who call themselves Christians are more zealous for convention than for conversion.

These men ask " *how* ? " but it is the *fact* and not the *means* that matters. I shall never know *how* I was converted, but I know that I am, and that is enough. The Pharisees and the people were divided in their opinion of Jesus, the former starting from their idea about the Sabbath, and the latter, from the fact of the healing: so appeal is made to the man for his opinion, and boldly did he give it—" *He is a prophet."* Do you stand your ground when pressed by the ungodly ?

Now the parents are called, and a miserable couple they are ; the son had not lost much all these years in not seeing them. They who should have been wild with joy, were filled with fear ; they were more concerned about the synagogue than salvation. And so the man is called again, but we shall consider his great testimony in the next portion.

Through all the ages Christ has been a subject of dispute, and concerning Him opinion has always been sharply divided. Ask yourself these two questions to-day—*What do I think of Christ?* and, *What does Christ think of me?*

Thought : *BE TRUE TO WHAT YOU KNOW OF CHRIST, HOWEVER LITTLE.*

ST. JOHN ix. 26-41

Title : *OUTSIDE THE CAMP WITH CHRIST*

26 Then said they to him again, What did he to thee ? how opened he thine eyes ?

27 He answered them, I have told you already, and ye did not hear : wherefore would ye hear it again ? will ye also be his disciples ?

28 Then they reviled him, and said, Thou art his disciple : but we are Moses' disciples. 29 We know that God spake unto Moses : as for this fellow, we know not from whence he is.

30 The man answered and said unto them, Why herein is a marvellous thing, that ye know not from whence he is, and yet he hath opened mine eyes. 31 Now we know that God heareth not sinners : but if any man be a worshipper of God, and doeth his will, him he heareth. 32 Since the world began was it not heard that any man opened the eyes of one that was born blind. 33 If this man were not of God, he could do nothing.

34 They answered and said unto him, Thou wast altogether born in sins, and dost thou teach us ? And they cast him out.

35 Jesus heard that they had cast him out ; and

when he had found him, he said unto him, Dost thou believe on the Son of God?

36 He answered and said, Who is he, Lord, that I might believe on him?

37 And Jesus said unto him, Thou hast both seen him, and it is he that talketh with thee.

38 And he said, Lord, I believe. And he worshipped him.

39 And Jesus said, For judgment I am come into this world, that they which see not might see; and that they which see might be made blind.

40 And some of the Pharisees which were with him heard these words, and said unto him, Are we blind also?

41 Jesus said unto them, If ye were blind, ye should have no sin: but now ye say, We see; therefore your sin remaineth.

EXPOSITION

We come now to the fourth of our divisions—

4. THE CONFESSION (24–33). The Pharisees wished to get this man to change his opinion about Jesus (17), and in the attempt exhibited their own dense darkness spiritually: "*give God the praise; we know that this man is a sinner*": but no one who dishonours the Son can honour the Father. The *knowledge* of some people is ignorance.

Now mark the healed man's reply (25). Over against their "we know," is his "I know." He really did know, and they did not. There is no better apologetic for Christianity than a well-saved soul. *Know* something, and let that knowledge be the child of experience. And knowing, tell what you know, and be sure and keep within the limits of your knowledge. Perhaps you will be abused and cast out (28, 35), but that is a small price to pay for sight.

There are always people who, when beaten on their merits, turn to throwing mud at their betters; but abuse is never argument. Tinker Bunyan and Cobbler Carey will be remembered while the world lasts, but their critics are forgotten overnight. How bold this man becomes, and what a flood of light is pouring into his soul as he goes (30–33).

5. THE PERSECUTION (34). What his parents feared (22), he got: but his excommunication was promotion: he went from the synagogue to the Saviour. It is better to be outside some churches than inside Laodicean churches, which keep Christ standing at the door without. Such is not a Christian Church, but only a Religious Club.

6. THE REVELATION (35-38). Truly *we shall know if we follow on to know the Lord*. If we be loyal to Christ so far as we know Him, we shall come to know Him better (xvii. 36). What began in *wonder* ended in *worship* (38).

7. THE CONDEMNATION (39-41). A bigot is like the pupil of the eye, the more light you pour upon it the more it contracts. Better is it to own to blindness and get sight, than to imagine we see and remain blind.

Thought: THOSE WHO ARE BLIND CANNOT SEE; BUT SOMETIMES THOSE WHO HAVE SIGHT DO NOT LOOK.

ST. JOHN x. 1-18

Title: THE DOOR AND THE SHEPHERD

1 Verily, verily, I say unto you, He that entereth not by the door into the sheepfold, but climbeth up some other way, the same is a thief and a robber. 2 But he that entereth in by the door is the shepherd of the sheep. 3 To him the porter openeth; and the sheep hear his voice: and he calleth his own sheep by name, and leadeth them out. 4 And when he putteth forth his own sheep, he goeth before them, and the sheep follow him: for they know his voice. 5 And a stranger will they not follow, but will flee from him: for they know not the voice of strangers.

6 This parable spake Jesus unto them: but they understood not what things they were which he spake unto them.

7 Then said Jesus unto them again, Verily, verily, I say unto you, I am the door of the sheep. 8 All that ever came before me are thieves and robbers: but the sheep did not hear them. 9 I am the door:

by me if any man enter in, he shall be saved, and shall go in and out, and find pasture. 10 The thief cometh not, but for to steal, and to kill, and to destroy : I am come that they might have life, and that they might have it more abundantly.

11 I am the good shepherd : the good shepherd giveth his life for the sheep. 12 But he that is an hireling, and not the shepherd, whose own the sheep are not, seeth the wolf coming, and leaveth the sheep, and fleeth : and the wolf catcheth them, and scattereth the sheep. 13 The hireling fleeth, because he is an hireling, and careth not for the sheep. 14 I am the good shepherd, and know my sheep, and am known of mine.

15 As the Father knoweth me, even so know I the Father : and I lay down my life for the sheep. 16 And other sheep I have, which are not of this fold : them also I must bring, and they shall hear my voice ; and there shall be one fold, and one shepherd. 17 Therefore doth my Father love me, because I lay down my life, that I might take it again. 18 No man taketh it from me, but, I lay it down of myself. I have power to lay it down, and I have power to take it again. This commandment have I received of my Father.

EXPOSITION

It is important to observe the connection between this and the previous chapter. By "*you*" in verse one are meant the Pharisees of ix. 39–41 ; so that verses 1–21 of our chapter record the discourse which arose immediately out of the miracle and its effects, of the previous chapter. There is here a double revelation.

1. THE DOOR REVELATION (1–10). This divides itself into Illustration (1–5) and Interpretation (6–10).

Under the (i) *Illustration*, attention is called first to *the shepherds and the porter* (1–3a) ; and then to *the Shepherd and the sheep* (3b–5). Take note of the figures in this allegory : the *fold*, the *door*, the *porter*, the *thief*, the *sheep*, the *shepherd*, the *hireling*, and the *wolf*. Christ is the *Door* in this story : who is the *porter* ? Who the *wolf* ? and who the *thief* ?

Now follows the (ii) *Interpretation* (6–10). Here

we are taught the *exclusiveness* of the Door (7-8), the *benefits* of it (9), and the *necessity* for it (10). There is only one Door of entrance into life, and he who enters finds freedom and provision (9). We are not called to a life anæmic and impotent, but to life *abounding* (10). Are you living victoriously ? Now comes—

2. THE SHEPHERD REVELATION (11-18), and Conclusion (19-21). Here is brought before us the relation of the Shepherd, first to the *Hireling* (11-13), then to the *Sheep* (14-16), and finally to the *Father* (17-18). The Shepherd saves the sheep, but the hireling abandons them. The shepherd will save them *all*, and at last there will be but *one flock* (16). The dominating thought in this part of the lesson is that *the Shepherd dies that His sheep might live* (11, 15, 17, 18). That is the heart of the gospel, and the declaration has always and will always cause a cleavage (19-21). Right and left, life and death, heaven and hell—these are the alternatives.

Thought : CHRIST'S DEATH WAS A GIFT (11). *HAVE YOU ACCEPTED IT ?*

ST. JOHN x. 19-30

Title : *ETERNAL SALVATION*

19 There was a division therefore again among the Jews for these sayings. 20 And many of them said, He hath a devil, and is mad ; why hear ye him ? 21 Others said, These are not the words of him that hath a devil. Can a devil open the eyes of the blind ?

22 And it was at Jerusalem the feast of the dedication, and it was winter. 23 And Jesus walked in the temple in Solomon's porch. 24 Then came the Jews round about him, and said unto him, How long dost thou make us to doubt ? If thou be the Christ, tell us plainly.

25 Jesus answered them, I told you, and ye believed not : the works that I do in my Father's name, they bear witness of me. 26 But ye believe not, because ye are not of my sheep, as I said unto

you. 27 My sheep hear my voice, and I know them, and they follow me : 28 And I give unto them eternal life ; and they shall never perish, neither shall any man pluck them out of my hand. 29 My Father, which gave them me, is greater than all ; and no man is able to pluck them out of my Father's hand. 30 I and my Father are one.

EXPOSITION

Let us again consider, for a moment, where we are in the main outline of the Book. Look once more at the outline in the portion John vii. 1–18 ; and observe that we are at the point of *The Love Outraged* (10), in the division The CONTROVERSY DEVELOPED (v. 19 to x. 42). How terrible an indictment of the people is this, that they *despised the Life, refused the Light, and outraged the Love* : people did it then, and people are doing it still.

These Jews were always trying to throw upon Jesus a responsibility which was their own. They attributed their uncertainty to His indefiniteness, instead of to their own stupidity (24) : but He faced them with two facts: His works, and their alienation (25, 26). When you hear the Shepherd, do you follow Him ? (27). One can hear without following, but no one can follow without hearing.

The 28th verse is one of the great utterances of the Gospel, but is liable to be misunderstood from opposite standpoints ; two truths therefore must be insisted upon—on the one hand that God's power is infinite and His promises certain ; and on the other hand, that " we cannot be protected against ourselves in spite of ourselves." He who ceases to hear and to follow is thereby shown to be no true believer (1 John ii. 19). No one who is not " *in His hand* " ever feared lest he should be " *plucked out of it.*" Some people want to be assured that they will not be eternally lost. That assurance can come only by knowing that you are eternally saved.

Whoever is in Christ's hand is also in the Father's hand (29), for Christ and the Father are one (30). The Greek language distinguishes gender in the case of the numeral, and it is most important to notice that "*one*" in this verse is "*neuter,*" and not *masculine* (hen, not heis). This fact shows that the Son and the Father are *not one person* but *one in essence and nature*.

Thought : WE MUST WORK OUT THE SALVA-
TION WHICH GOD WORKS IN.

ST. JOHN x. 31-42

Title : THE CHRIST, THE SON OF GOD

31 Then the Jews took up stones again to stone him.
32 Jesus answered them, Many good works have I shewed you from my Father ; for which of those works do ye stone me ?
33 The Jews answered him, saying, For a good work we stone thee not ; but for blasphemy ; and because that thou, being a man, makest thyself God.
34 Jesus answered them, Is it not written in your law, I said, Ye are gods ? 35 If he called them gods, unto whom the word of God came, and the scripture cannot be broken ; 36 Say ye of him, whom the Father hath sanctified, and sent into the world, Thou blasphemest ; because I said, I am the Son of God ? 37 If I do not the works of my Father, believe me not. 38 But if I do, though ye believe not me, believe the works : that ye may know, and believe, that the Father is in me, and I in him.
39 Therefore they sought again to take him : but he escaped out of their hand, 40 And went away again beyond Jordan into the place where John at first baptized ; and there he abode. 41 And many resorted unto him, and said, John did no miracle : but all things that John spake of this man were true. 42 And many believed on him there.

EXPOSITION

The whole section 22-39, should be carefully read again, because the subject is one, and the argument is cumulative in its force. Two facts dominate the discussion ; first, that the Jews were not wholly indisposed to see in Jesus the Messiah of prophecy (24); and second, that He definitely claimed to be the Son of God, a claim which the Jews considered blasphemy (30, 33). This shows that the Jews had not read aright their own Scriptures. For they did not know that the promised Messiah was the Son of God.

Christ's claim to Deity in this discussion should be carefully considered ; also the ground or evidence of it, His miracles. Well, because the Jews did not and could not understand, Christ's claim, they thought they had better get rid of Him (31). Now stone-throwing was never an argument, but the stupid resort of those who never had any ground, intellectual or moral, for the attitude they assumed to Christ and His disciples. But when you have got rid of a witness to the truth, *you have not got rid of the truth* : from the ground it blossoms red, red with the blood of the faithful. It is better to think sanely than to throw stones.

The only ground on which we have a right to deny Christ's claim for Himself, is that of positive disproof of it. Very many reject Christ's claim, but not all (42). There always have been some who hearing have heeded His word. Are you one of them ? It will be well for us who are preachers if, when souls come to the Saviour, they are able to say that all we told them of Him was true (41). A salvation-preacher is better than a sign-producer. It is better to get people to gaze at Christ than get them to gaze at us.

Thought : FAITH IS MORE FORCEFUL THAN FEROCITY.

ST. JOHN xi. 1-16

Title : *WAITING TO BE GRACIOUS*

1 Now a certain man was sick, named Lazarus, of Bethany, the town of Mary and her sister Martha. 2 (It was that Mary which anointed the Lord with ointment, and wiped his feet with her hair, whose brother Lazarus was sick). 3 Therefore his sisters

sent unto him, saying, Lord, behold, he whom thou lovest is sick.

4 When Jesus heard that, he said, This sickness is not unto death, but for the glory of God, that the Son of God might be glorified thereby. 5 Now Jesus loved Martha, and her sister, and Lazarus. 6 When he had heard therefore that he was sick, he abode two days still in the same place where he was.

7 Then after that saith he to his disciples, Let us go into Judæa again. 8 His disciples say unto him, Master, the Jews of late sought to stone thee; and goest thou hither again?

9 Jesus answered, Are there not twelve hours in the day? If any man walk in the day, he stumbleth not, because he seeth the light of this world. 10 But if a man walk in the night, he stumbleth, because there is no light in him.

11 These things said he: and after that he saith unto them, Our friend Lazarus sleepeth; but I go, that I may awake him out of sleep. 12 Then said his disciples, Lord, if he sleep, he shall do well. 13 Howbeit Jesus spake of his death: but they thought that he had spoken of taking of rest in sleep. 14 Then said Jesus unto them plainly, Lazarus is dead. 15 And I am glad for your sakes that I was not there, to the intent ye may believe; nevertheless let us go unto him.

16 Then said Thomas, which is called Didymus, unto his fellow-disciples, Let us also go, that we may die with him.

EXPOSITION

This is a great chapter, and for a moment we must look at it as a whole. Between chapters x. and xi. of this Gospel comes Luke xi. 1 to xvii. 10: and the events recorded in John xi, come in between verses 10 and 11 of Luke xvii. THE RAISING OF LAZARUS is the seventh miracle recorded by this evangelist. What are the previous six? The controversy which was *aroused* in v. 1–18, and *developed* in v. 19, to x. 42, is here *concluded* (xi and xii): and in this conclusion we are made to see THE LOVE SYMPATHIZING (xi. 1–37), THE LIFE SAVING (xi. 38–xii. 11), and THE LIGHT SHINING (xii. 12–50).

Our chapter falls into four principal parts, around the miracle—the Occasion of it (1–16); the Approach to it (17–32); the Performance of it (33–44); and the Consequences of it (45–57). Mark these in the margin of your Bible.

1. THE OCCASION OF THE MIRACLE (1–16). It was the sickness eventuating in the death of Lazarus, one of Jesus' intimate friends. Do *you* instinctively turn to Jesus when you are in trouble? (1–3). How amazing are verses 5, 6! We would have supposed that upon receiving this news Jesus would have departed at once for Bethany; but He would have us learn that *delay* is neither *destitution* (4), nor *desertion* (5, 6), nor *denial* (7). The divine love sometimes lingers. When God waits, we should wait.

How astonishing also is the dullness of the disciples (11–13)? Does Christ find us stupid when He talks to us? When there was a grave to be emptied, hearts to be gladdened, and God to be glorified, stones could not keep Jesus back (7–10). The higher knowledge is only for the spiritual mind. Where there is a want of insight, meanings must be spelt out, like words to a child (14). Faith is aided in strange ways betimes (15). How many living hours are there in your day? (9).

Thought: *FELLOWS IN THE FIGHT, FACE UP* (16).

ST. JOHN xi. 17-31

Title: *MARTHA RECEIVES A REVELATION*

17 Then when Jesus came, he found that he had laid in the grave four days already. **18** Now Bethany was nigh unto Jerusalem, about fifteen furlongs off. **19** And many of the Jews came to Martha and Mary, to comfort them concerning their brother.

20 Then Martha, as soon as she heard that Jesus was coming, went and met him; but Mary sat still in the house. **21** Then said Martha unto Jesus, Lord, if thou hadst been here, my brother had not died. **22** But I know, that even now, whatsoever thou wilt ask of God, God will give it thee.

23 Jesus saith unto her, Thy brother shall rise again.

24 Martha saith unto him, I know that he shall rise again in the resurrection at the last day.

25 Jesus said unto her, I am the resurrection and the life : he that believeth in me, though he were dead, yet shall he live : 26 And whosoever liveth and believeth in me shall never die. Believest thou this ?

27 She saith unto him, Yea, Lord : I believe that thou art the Christ, the Son of God, which should come into the world. 28 And when she had so said, she went her way, and called Mary her sister secretly, saying, The Master is come, and calleth for thee. 29 As soon as she heard that, she arose quickly, and came unto him.

30 Now Jesus was not yet come into the town, but was in that place where Martha met him. 31 The Jews then which were with her in the house, and comforted her, when they saw Mary, that she rose up hastily and went out, followed her, saying, She goeth unto the grave to weep there.

EXPOSITION

See the outline in the preceding portion.

2. THE APPROACH TO THE MIRACLE (17–32). We have in this chapter a profoundly interesting study of these two sisters, with which you should read Luke x. 38–42. In the latter passage Jesus is not elevating the *contemplative* above the *practical* : Mary *did* as well as *thought*, but Martha *thought* less than she *did*. Their characteristics come out in our lesson (20).

How greatly disappointed must these sisters have been that Jesus had not arrived in time to prevent Lazarus dying (21) ; yet, they who had looked to Him for *cure* now look to Him for *comfort* (20). Martha's disappointment had not killed her faith (22), though it is not quite clear what she was expecting Jesus to do, for, from what follows, it would seem that any thought of a miracle was not in her mind (24).

It should not be overlooked that at this time

Martha did not know that her dear friend was the Son of God. The evidence of this is not in verse 27 only, but in the word "*ask*," which she uses in verse 22, a word which is used in the New Testament of our prayers, but never of Christ's (cf. Gr. *aiteō*, and *erōtaō*).

How often has trouble issued in revelation (25)! We had never seen the rainbow but for the storm. Mark what Christ says (25, 26) and then answer His question put to you, "*believest thou this?*" Martha expected something from Christ, but He gives Himself to her. The highest truth is not that He *has* what we need, but that He *is* what we need. He points, not to some future gift, but to a present grace; not to a blessing, but to Himself the Blessing. "*I am the Resurrection and the Life.*" He Who quickens raises. The living should not live in a grave. I wonder how much we really believe! Martha's little faith became much (27); her sad heart was ready to receive this great word; and she went forthwith and called Mary. Notice what she said, "the *Master*" (28). Yes, He is ever coming and calling: He is coming to you and calling for you now. Listen! Do you hear Him?

Thought: HOW GREAT A THING IS A LOVING FAMILY!

ST. JOHN xi. 32-46

Title: VICTORY OVER DEATH AND THE GRAVE

32 Then when Mary was come where Jesus was, and saw him, she fell down at his feet, saying unto him, Lord, if thou hadst been here, my brother had not died.
33 When Jesus therefore saw her weeping, and the Jews also weeping which came with her, he groaned in the spirit, and was troubled, 34 And said, Where have ye laid him? They said unto him, Lord, come and see. 35 Jesus wept.
36 Then said the Jews, Behold how he loved him!

37 And some of them said, Could not this man, which opened the eyes of the blind, have caused that even this man should not have died?

38 Jesus therefore again groaning in himself cometh to the grave. It was a cave, and a stone lay upon it. 39 Jesus said, Take ye away the stone. Martha, the sister of him that was dead, saith unto him, Lord, by this time he stinketh: for he hath been dead four days. 40 Jesus saith unto her, Said I not unto thee, that, if thou wouldest believe, thou shouldest see the glory of God! 41 Then they took away the stone from the place where the dead was laid. And Jesus lifted up his eyes, and said, Father, I thank thee that thou hast heard me. 42 And I knew that thou hearest me always: but because of the people which stand by I said it, that they may believe that thou hast sent me. 43 And when he thus had spoken, he cried with a loud voice, Lazarus, come forth. 44 And he that was dead came forth, bound hand and foot with graveclothes; and his face was bound about with a napkin. Jesus saith unto them, Loose him, and let him go.

45 Then many of the Jews which came to Mary, and had seen the things which Jesus did, believed on him. 46 But some of them went their ways to the Pharisees, and told them what things Jesus had done.

EXPOSITION

For the connection see the outline on the portion John xi. 1–16.

3. THE PERFORMANCE OF THE MIRACLE (33–44). The first thing to note here is *Jesus' grief* (33–38). He Who was joyful in the shadow of His own cross, is sorrowful at the mouth of some one else's grave. Only those capable of exquisite sorrow can experience " joy unspeakable "; depth is height.

Jesus' intention to raise Lazarus immediately did not make His sorrow less. He genuinely sorrowed with these two women who were His friends, but the deepest ground of His grief was in His knowledge that by sin came death; and that fact led Him perhaps to anticipate Calvary. Christ ever had and has " a heart at leisure from itself to sooth and sympathise." Are you in trouble to-day ? He is beside you, and He cares.

Some people are so insensible that they will grumble even at the grave (37); yet these, in doing so, recalled a great miracle (ch. 9). *" Could He not ? "* (37). Oh, yes ; but He never did all He could, but only what He would for the good of men and the glory of God.

The second thing to note is, *the immediate preparation for the miracle* (39-42). Jesus was about to do what those there could not do, but He will not do what they can (39). Remember that will you, and this very day answer some of your own prayers. The Son here does not *ask* anything of the Father, but *thanks* Him for prayer already answered (41, 42, 4). Do you ever do that ?

The third thing to note is, *the raising of Lazarus* (43, 44). The great notes are—*dead, alive, bound, free*. If all bound Christians were to get set free from their grave-clothes, the world would sit up and look, and listen, as it has never done. Are you an enslaved Christian ? Can you say,

" I never thought it could be thus,
  Month after month to know
The river of Thy peace without
  A ripple in its flow,
Without a quiver in the trust,
  A flicker in the glow " ?
But I have found it so.

Thought : HE WHO CAN RAISE US FROM DEATH CAN RELEASE US FROM SIN.

ST. JOHN xi. 47-57

Title : *CAIAPHAS AND CHRIST*

47 Then gathered the chief priests and the Pharisees a council, and said, What do we ? for this man doeth many miracles. 48 If we let him thus alone, all men will believe on him : and the Romans shall come and take away both our place and nation.

49 And one of them, named Caiaphas, being the high priest that same year, said unto them, Ye know nothing at all, 50 Nor consider that it is expedient for us, that one man should die for the people, and that the whole nation perish not. 51 And this spake he not of himself; but being high priest that year, he prophesied that Jesus should die for that nation; 52 And not for that nation only, but that also he should gather together in one the children of God that were scattered abroad.

53 Then from that day forth they took counsel together for to put him to death. 54 Jesus therefore walked no more openly among the Jews; but went thence unto a country near to the wilderness, into a city called Ephraim, and there continued with his disciples.

55 And the Jews' passover was nigh at hand: and many went out of the country up to Jerusalem before the passover, to purify themselves. 56 Then sought they for Jesus, and spake among themselves, as they stood in the temple, What think ye, that he will not come to the feast? 57 Now both the chief priests and the Pharisees had given a commandment, that, if any man knew where he were, he should shew it, that they might take him.

EXPOSITION

See the outline in the portion John xi. 1-16.

4. THE CONSEQUENCES OF THE MIRACLE (45-47). These are stated in three paragraphs.

FIRST, there is *a division of opinion* (45, 46), which represents faith (45) and unbelief (46). It always has been so. When Christ passes by, you must stand on the right hand, or on the left.

SECOND, *the Sanhedrin commit themselves* (47-53). There is a tragic humour in what these officials said (47, 48). They admitted much, anticipated more, and argued badly: observe these three things. But Caiaphas comes to the rescue. Not for a moment must it be supposed either that Caiaphas had any sympathy with Jesus, or that he understood the full significance of what he said (50). He offered counsel which was bold and unprincipled, to this effect, that by making a victim of Jesus they may hope not only to avert a popular rising, but also to show their zeal for the honour of Caesar. Thus did he hide self-interest under the cloak of patriotism. Verse 52 is John's expansion of the meaning latent in the words of Caiaphas.

The time when this Council met was a memorable day (53) in a memorable *year* (49, 51); and John could not forget either. Will this year be memorable because of some great failure, or some great success of yours?

THIRD, *we see both parties standing by* (54-57), Jesus and His disciples at Ephraim, and the Jews at Jerusalem; it was a season of suspense. These men were going, so they thought, to put an end to Jesus (53). As well try to put out the sun by blowing at it. As well try to keep back the up-rushing tide with a broom. Nothing is so impotent as infidelity. "*To purify themselves*" indeed! (55). Remember, you do not clean your heart when you wash your hands. A pure skin is of little consequence if it covers an unclean soul. Get thee to the Fountain just now.

Thought: *THE SCHEMES OF MEN CAN NEVER FRUSTRATE THE PURPOSE OF GOD.*

ST. JOHN xii. 1-19

Title: *LOVE AND HATE*

1 Then Jesus six days before the passover came to Bethany, where Lazarus was which had been dead, whom he raised from the dead. 2 There they made him a supper; and Martha served: but Lazarus was one of them that sat at the table with him.

3 Then took Mary a pound of ointment of spikenard, very costly, and anointed the feet of Jesus, and wiped his feet with her hair: and the house was filled with the odour of the ointment. 4 Then saith one of his disciples, Judas Iscariot, Simon's son, which should betray him, 5 Why was not this ointment sold for three hundred pence, and given to the poor? 6 This he said, not that he cared for

the poor ; but because he was a thief, and had the bag, and bare what was put therein.

7 Then said Jesus, Let her alone : against the day of my burying hath she kept this. 8 For the poor always ye have with you ; but me ye have not always.

9 Much people of the Jews, therefore knew that he was there : and they came not for Jesus' sake only, but that they might see Lazarus also, whom he had raised from the dead.

10 But the chief priests consulted that they might put Lazarus also to death ; 11 Because that by reason of him many of the Jews went away, and believed on Jesus.

12 On the next day much people that were come to the feast, when they heard that Jesus was coming to Jerusalem, 13 Took branches of palm trees, and went forth to meet him, and cried, Hosanna : Blessed is the King of Israel that cometh in the name of the Lord. 14 And Jesus, when he had found a young ass, sat thereon ; as it is written, 15 Fear not, daughter of Sion : behold, thy King cometh, sitting on an ass's colt. 16 These things understood not his disciples at the first : but when Jesus was glorified, then remembered they that these things were written of him, and that they had done these things unto him.

17 The people therefore that was with him when he called Lazarus out of his grave, and raised him from the dead, bare record. 18 For this cause the people also met him, for that they heard that he had done this miracle. 19 The Pharisees therefore said among themselves, Perceive ye how ye prevail nothing ? behold, the world is gone after him.

EXPOSITION

As we take up this chapter for our meditation, it will be meet for us to glance it down at once, and get a general idea of what it is about. We shall find that it is in five sections as follows : 1. *Jesus and the Disciples* (1–11). 2. *Jesus and the Multitude* (12–19). 3. *Jesus and the World* (20–36a). 4. *John's Verdict on Jesus' Work* (36b–43). 5. *Jesus' Verdict on His own Work* (44–50). Look now at the first two of these.

1. JESUS AND THE DISCIPLES (1-11). Mark these three points: (i) *The Feast at Bethany* (1-2). The miracle on Lazarus strikes four great notes relative to the Christian life—*death, life, liberty,* and *fellowship* (xi. 41-44; xii. 1-2). How far have you got in this programme? Remember, even where there is *life* there is not true *fellowship* where there is not *liberty*. Get *loosed* to-day.

(ii) *The Ointment and the Objection* (3-8). Have you ever done anything " *very costly* " (3) for your Lord? If you have, I am certain that some one objected. They do not talk about " *waste* " when, at the risk of almost certain death, men and women try to fly the Atlantic, but they are loud about " waste " when for the cause of Christ, at home and abroad, men and women gladly lay down their lives! Have nothing to do with the Judas cult. If the Master endorses your action you need not mind what others say about you (7-8).

(iii) *Insensate Hate* (9-11). All through the ages this method has been in vogue, namely, if you cannot invalidate Christian testimony, get rid of the witness: but truth has never suffered because of rack and stake. Truth must prevail; the right always wins.

2. JESUS AND THE MULTITUDE (12-19). There is something sad about this welcome given to the Christ, for too soon the crown was of thorns. It is always easier to shout for Christ with the crowd, than to stand alone for Him at the Cross.

They said, " *the world is gone after Him* " (19). Would that it were so; it would be nearer the truth if Christians were more like Christ.

Thought: *GIVE TO CHRIST WHAT COSTS YOU SOMETHING.*

ST. JOHN xii. 20-36

Title: *LIFE BY DEATH*

20 And there were certain Greeks among them that came up to worship at the feast: 21 The same

came therefore to Philip, which was of Bethsaida of Galilee, and desired him, saying, Sir, we would see Jesus. 22 Philip cometh and telleth Andrew: and again Andrew and Philip tell Jesus.

23 And Jesus answered them, saying, The hour is come, that the Son of man should be glorified. 24 Verily, verily, I say unto you, Except a corn of wheat fall into the ground and die, it abideth alone: but if it die, it bringeth forth much fruit. 25 He that loveth his life shall lose it; and he that hateth his life in this world shall keep it unto life eternal. 26 If any man serve me, let him follow me; and where I am, there shall also my servant be: if any man serve me, him will my Father honour. 27 Now is my soul troubled; and what shall I say? Father, save me from this hour: but for this cause came I unto this hour. 28 Father, glorify thy name. Then came there a voice from heaven, saying, I have both glorified it, and will glorify it again.

29 The people therefore, that stood by, and heard it, said that it thundered: others said, An angel spake to him.

30 Jesus answered and said, This voice came not because of me, but for your sakes. 31 Now is the judgment of this world: now shall the prince of this world be cast out. 32 And I, if I be lifted up from the earth, will draw all men unto me. 33 This he said, signifying what death he should die.

34 The people answered him, We have heard out of the law that Christ abideth for ever: and how sayest thou, The Son of man must be lifted up? who is this Son of man?

35 Then Jesus said unto them, Yet a little while is the light with you. Walk while ye have the light, lest darkness come upon you: for he that walketh in darkness knoweth not whither he goeth. 36 While ye have light, believe in the light, that ye may be the children of light. These things spake Jesus, and departed, and did hide himself from them.

EXPOSITION

Connect from the preceding outline.

3. JESUS AND THE WORLD. In this momentous incident are five paragraphs.

(i) *The Vision* (20–22). In the Court of the Temple certain " proselytes of the gate " ask for and obtain an interview with Jesus. What they said is unrecorded, but we may infer what it was from Christ's answer to them. The substance of it would appear to have been,—" your own people have rejected you ; we will receive you ; come with us."

(ii) *The Reckoning* (23–26). How profound is this *answer*, first the declaration (23), then the illustration (24), and finally the application (25, 26). Fruit is by *dying* not by *doing* : sacrifice is the secret of productiveness : this is true in the realms of the *soil* and of the *soul*. Christ applies this truth both to Himself (25) and His disciples (26).

(iii) *The Conflict* (27–30). This is luminous if we read verses 27, 28, in this way : " *What shall I say ? Shall I say, ' Father save me from this hour ? ' But for this cause came I unto this hour ! No, I will say, ' Father glorify Thy Name.' *" His rescue would have been our ruin ; but His death has brought our deliverance. The Father bore witness to His Son three times, at His Baptism, on the Mount of Transfiguration, and here (28). Alas, that still so little is the Divine Voice recognised that it is thought to be a tone of nature, or perchance, an angelic sound (29).

(iv) *The Triumph* (31–33). Verse 32 is one of the greatest in the Bible. Christ's sovereignty is by His sacrifice. *"All"* means, without distinction, not, without exception. Christ is the Great Magnet. Spurgeon says that He draws like a Trumpet, like a Net, like a Cord, like a Standard, and like a Chariot. Has He drawn you ?

(v) *The Warning* (34–36a). Here are REVELATION, *" ye have "* ; APPREHENSION, *" believe "* ; and TRANSFORMATION, *" become "* (36).

This portion plainly sets before us the philosophy of salvation, which, for the head is *knowledge*, but for the heart is *wisdom*.

Thought : THE GORY CROSS WAS GLORIOUS.

ST. JOHN xii. 37-50

Title : BELIEF AND UNBELIEF

37 But though he had done so many miracles before them, yet they believed not on him : 38 That the saying of Esaias the prophet might be fulfilled, which he spake, Lord, who hath believed our report and to whom hath the arm of the Lord been revealed ? 39 Therefore they could not believe, because that Esaias said again, 40 He hath blinded their eyes, and hardened their heart ; that they should not see with their eyes, nor understand with their heart, and be converted, and I should heal them. 41 These things said Esaias, when he saw his glory, and spake of him.

42 Nevertheless among the chief rulers also many believed on him ; but because of the Pharisees they did not confess him, lest they should be put out of the synagogue : 43 For they loved the praise of men more than the praise of God.

44 Jesus cried and said, He that believeth on me, believeth not on me, but on him that sent me. 45 And he that seeth me seeth him that sent me. 46 I am come a light into the world, that whosoever believeth on me should not abide in darkness. 47 And if any man hear my words, and believe not, I judge him not : for I came not to judge the world, but to save the world. 48 He that rejecteth me, and receiveth not my words, hath one that judgeth him : the word that I have spoken, the same shall judge him in the last day. 49 For I have not spoken of myself : but the Father which sent me, he gave me a commandment, what I should say, and what I should speak. 50 And I know that his commandment is life everlasting : whatsoever I speak therefore, even as the Father said unto me, so I speak.

EXPOSITION

4. JOHN'S VERDICT ON JESUS' WORK (36b–43 : see outline on chapter xii. 1–19). We all and all the time are under the necessity of forming judgments, even if we do not pronounce verdicts. The Apostle John in this passage, and after the lapse of sixty years, records what he remembers of the effect of his Master's ministry. That effect was two-fold ;

"*they believed not on Him*" (37), and "*many believed on Him*" (42). There are always these issues from the preaching of the Gospel.

By verse 38, we are not to imagine that these people did not believe, in order to fulfil a prophecy, but that in not believing they did in fact fulfil it. Both quotations here (38, 40) are from "Isaiah," the first, from the second part (chs. 40-66), and the second from the first part (1-39). Both are attributed to the prophet.

Unbelief is not compulsory but voluntary: they "*could not*" because they would not; their state was due to their own *attitude*, and not to the Divine *action*. It is important also to observe that "*the Lord*" Whom Isaiah "*saw sitting upon a throne*" (Isa. vi. 1) was CHRIST (41). Mark also the poorness of these people's faith (42, 43). What do *you* love most?

5. JESUS' VERDICT ON HIS OWN WORK (44-50). In verse 44-46, Jesus speaks of His *Person*, and of those who *believe*. In verses 47-50, He speaks of His *Words*, and of those who *believe not*. No one can have faith in His Person who rejects His testimony. *His word shall judge us* (48) who judge His word. His word comes with absolute authority. Westcott says of verse 49, "*of myself*"; "the phrase is peculiar and unique. It describes, so to speak, the source out of which a stream flows continually, and not simply the point of origin from which movement started."

"*I know . . . I speak.*" Every one who is *speaking* to-day does not *know*. When Christ speaks—listen, because He knows.

Thought : *CHRIST IS THE CRITIC AND HIS CROSS IS THE CRUX.*

ST. JOHN xiii. 1-17

Title : *THE SOVEREIGNTY OF SERVICE*

1 Now before the feast of the passover, when Jesus knew that his hour was come that he should depart out of this world unto the Father, having loved his own which were in the world, he loved them unto the end. 2 And supper being ended, the devil having now put into the heart of Judas Iscariot, Simon's son, to betray him ; 3 Jesus knowing that the Father had given all things into his hands, and that he was come from God, and went to God ; 4 He riseth from supper, and laid aside his garments ; and took a towel, and girded himself. 5 After that he poured water into a bason, and began to wash the disciples' feet, and to wipe them with the towel wherewith he was girded.

6 Then cometh he to Simon Peter ; and Peter saith unto him, Lord, dost thou wash my feet ?

7 Jesus answered and said unto him, What I do thou knowest not now ; but thou shalt know hereafter.

8 Peter saith unto him, Thou shalt never wash my feet.

Jesus answered him, If I wash thee not, thou hast no part with me.

9 Simon Peter saith unto him, Lord, not my feet only, but also my hands and my head.

10 Jesus saith to him, He that is washed needeth not save to wash his feet, but is clean every whit : and ye are clean, but not all. 11 For he knew who should betray him ; therefore said he, Ye are not all clean.

12 So after he had washed their feet, and had taken his garments, and was set down again, he said unto them, Know ye what I have done to you ? 13 Ye call me Master and Lord : and ye say well ; for so I am. 14 If I then, your Lord and Master, have washed your feet ; ye also ought to wash one another's feet. 15 For I have given you an example, that ye should do as I have done to you. 16 Verily, verily, I say unto you, The servant is not greater than his lord ; neither he that is sent greater than he that sent him. 17 If ye know these things, happy are ye if ye do them.

EXPOSITION

Our portion falls into four parts : THE SETTING OF THE ACT (1–3) ; THE CHARACTER OF THE ACT (4, 5) ; THE SIGNIFICANCE OF THE ACT (6–11) ; and THE MORAL OF THE ACT (12–17). The great object of this story is to show how unchristian Christians may become Christ-like.

Think first of *Unchristian Christians*. We learn from verse 2, that the Supper had begun, and yet the feet of the disciples had not been washed. In the East this was usually done before men sat down to eat. Why, on this occasion, was it not done? For answer see Luke xxii. 24–30. The disciples had been so occupied disputing who should be the greatest that even the common decencies had been neglected; and now, what they should have done for Christ, He has to do, or rather, chooses to do for them.

Think of it! *Christians* scrambling for places and wrangling about honours in the shadow of the Cross! Have you ever done that? Are you doing it now? Do you seek and take office in the church just because of the prominence that it will give you? And do you refuse service which would leave you obscure?

Now, look at the other side,—*Christlike Christians*. How? Not by *pride*, but by *humility*; not by *getting*, but by *giving*: not by *ease*, but by *sacrifice*. The example of Christ is always offered in connection with some form of self-sacrifice. Many claim to be Christ's *disciples* who do not *follow* Him. To us all He is ever saying, " Because I did ... ye ought to do " (14). True *knowledge* leads to *action* which begets *joy*: " if ye *know* these things, *happy* are ye if ye *do* them " (17). Knowledge, Action, and Experience are vitally connected. What God hath joined together let not man put assunder.

At the beginning (Genesis iii) *man* wanted to become a *god*: at the end, *God* became a *servant*.

Thought: BEWARE OF SATAN AT THE SUPPER.

ST. JOHN xiii. 18-30

Title: JUDAS

18 I speak not of you all: I know whom I have chosen: but that the scripture may be fulfilled, He that eateth bread with me hath lifted up his heel

against me. 19 Now I tell you before it come, that, when it is come to pass, ye may believe that I am he. 20 Verily, verily, I say unto you, He that receiveth whomsoever I send receiveth me ; and he that receiveth me receiveth him that sent me.

21 When Jesus had thus said, he was troubled in spirit, and testified, and said, Verily, verily, I say unto you, that one of you shall betray me.

22 Then the disciples looked one on another, doubting of whom he spake.

23 Now there was leaning on Jesus' bosom one of his disciples, whom Jesus loved. 24 Simon Peter therefore beckoned to him, that he should ask who it should be of whom he spake. 25 He then lying on Jesus' breast saith unto him, Lord, who is it ?

26 Jesus answered, He it is, to whom I shall give a sop, when I have dipped it. And when he had dipped the sop, he gave it to Judas Iscariot, the son of Simon. 27 And after the sop Satan entered into him. Then said Jesus unto him, That thou doest, do quickly.

28 Now no man at the table knew for what intent he spake this unto him. 29 For some of them thought, because Judas had the bag, that Jesus had said unto him, Buy those things that we have need of against the feast ; or, that he should give something to the poor. 30 He then having received the sop went immediately out : and it was night.

EXPOSITION

Remember that this Record is in three main parts. We have considered—I. THE REVELATION OF THE SON TO THE WORLD AS LIFE (i. 19 to xii. 50). We are now considering—II. THE REVELATION OF THE SON TO THE DISCIPLES AS LIGHT (xiii to xvii). This part of the Gospel is its very heart, and is precious beyond all estimate. The Apostle John alone records these events and sayings.

The division has three sections : 1. *Introduction to the Light for them* (xiii. 1–30). 2. *Impartation of the Light to them* (xiii. 31–xvi. 33). 3. *Intercession for the Light in them* (xvii). In the preceding portion (xiii. 1–17) we considered the significance of the *Feet Washing* act. Now we are to listen to *Conversations at the Supper-table* (18–30). Verse 12, tells us that the Master has again taken His seat, and what He said is recorded in verses 12–17. You will observe that it is a lesson on *the self-sacrifice of love*, based upon the act of verses 2–11.

He intimates that there is schism in the circle, and He would have them know it before it becomes self-evident, that later on they may think of Him in the light of the forecast (18–20). Now a dark cloud comes over His spirit, and He speaks of *betrayal*. In answer to a question put by John at Peter's instigation, the charge is brought closer home (21–26), and still more closely when Jesus addresses Judas (27).

But, we are told, the disciples did not know why Judas left the table (29–30). Judas is an utter enigma, a tragic mystery. Mercifully he did not partake of the Lord's Supper, which was instituted after he had left. When Judas went out " *it was night* " (30). It always is when one goes away from Christ, because He is the Light. Out of that darkness Judas has never come.

The lesson should lead us to self-examination, lest we become worldly-minded and betray our Lord. To you and to me He says, " be thou faithful unto death, and I will give thee a crown of life."

Thought : DISLOYALTY IS TREACHERY.

ST. JOHN xiii. 31-38

Title : SAD NEWS

31 Therefore, when he was gone out, Jesus said, Now is the Son of man glorified, and God is glorified in him. 32 If God be glorified in him, God shall also glorify him in himself, and shall straightway glorify him. 33 Little children, yet a little while I am with you. Ye shall seek me : and as I said unto the Jews, Whither I go, ye cannot come ; so now I say to you. 34 A new commandment I give unto you, That ye love one another ; as I have loved you, that ye also love one another. 35 By this shall all men know that ye are my disciples, if ye have love one to another.

36 Simon Peter said unto him, Lord whither goest thou?

Jesus answered him, Whither I go, thou canst not follow me now; but thou shalt follow me afterwards.

37 Peter said unto him, Lord, why cannot I follow thee now? I will lay down my life for thy sake.

38 Jesus answered him, Wilt thou lay down thy life for my sake? Verily, verily, I say unto thee, The cock shall not crow, till thou hast denied me thrice.

EXPOSITION

After 1. *Introduction to the Light for the Disciples* (xiii. 1–30), is, *Impartation of the Light to them* (xiii. 31, to xvi. 33). This impartation of light is in our Lord's two discourses, one *in the Upper Room* (xiii. 31, to xiv. 31), and the other *on the way to the Garden* (xv. 1, to xvi. 33). The first discourse is *dialogue*; the second is *monologue*. In the first, JESUS replies to *Peter* (xiii. 36), to *Thomas* (xiv. 5), to *Philip* (xiv. 8), and to *Jude* (xiv. 22).

The subject in this portion is, THE COMING SEPARATION. Observe (i) *The Declaration* (31–33). " *Now* " in verse 31, is a note of relief consequent upon the exit of Judas, and introduces a song of " *glory*," present and to come (the word occurs five times here). The Master talked about glory in the deepest gloom; about love in time of fiercest hate; and about joy in the hour of most poignant sorrow. That is victory. He then tells of His coming departure introducing the painful subject with the tender " *little children*." Jesus prepares His disciples for the coming change; He always was perfectly frank with them, and is with us. But beyond the sad news was good news, as we shall see. The final revelation is sunrise, not sunset.

(ii) *The Command* (34–35). In these chapters (xiii to xvi) there are at least 26 references to " *love*." This is the new, the inclusive, and the final law of life. Read and memorise 1 Cor. xiii. Have we ever loved one another *as* He has loved us? (34). What

95

does the world think of Christians to-day ? (35). Of course its estimate and verdict may be, and often is, entirely wrong, but at times it is uncommonly shrewd and perfectly right. Don't let Christ down before His enemies.

(iii). *The Warning* (36–38). Of course it is *Peter* who speaks first, and he does so characteristically. Peter said, " I'll die." Jesus said, " No, you'll deny." Fleshly confidence is very near to well-nigh fatal apostasy. Our safest place is lying low at our Redeemer's feet.

Thought : LOVE IS THE ONLY TRUE LOYALTY.

ST. JOHN xiv. 1-14

Title : QUESTIONS AND ANSWERS

1 Let not your heart be troubled : ye believe in God, believe also in me. 2 In my Father's house are many mansions : if it were not so, I would have told you. I go to prepare a place for you. 3 And if I go and prepare a place for you, I will come again, and receive you unto myself ; that where I am, there ye may be also. 4 And whither I go ye know, and the way ye know.

5 Thomas saith unto him, Lord, we know not whither thou goest ; and how can we know the way ?

6 Jesus saith unto him, I am the way, the truth, and the life : no man cometh unto the Father, but by me. 7 If ye had known me, ye should have known my Father also : and from henceforth ye know him, and have seen him.

8 Philip saith unto him, Lord, show us the Father, and it sufficeth us.

9 Jesus saith unto him, Have I been so long time with you, and yet hast thou not known me, Philip ? he that hath seen me hath seen the Father ; and how sayest thou then, Shew us the Father ? 10 Believest thou not that I am in the Father, and the Father in me ? the words that I speak unto you I speak not of myself : but the Father that dwelleth in me, he doeth the works. 11 Believe me that I am in the Father, and the Father in me : or else believe me for the very works' sake.

12 Verily, verily, I say unto you, He that believeth on me, the works that I do shall he do also ; and greater works than these shall he do ; because I go unto my Father. **13** And whatsoever ye shall ask in my name, that will I do, that the Father may be glorified in the Son. **14** If ye shall ask any thing in my name, I will do it.

EXPOSITION

The FIRST DISCOURSE in this division of John's Gospel is *Dialogue* (xiii. 31, to xiv. 31). Let us mark this in fuller detail.

FIRST DIALOGUE: PETER and JESUS (xiii. 31, to xiv. 4). *Peter's Inquiry*: " Where art Thou going, and why cannot I follow Thee now ? " *Jesus' Reply*: " There are discipline and design in my departure." The *discipline* we have already considered: the *design* is revealed here. Christ went "*to prepare a place*" for us. How did He do this ? By, as Man, opening Heaven for believing men. The " *mansions* " are in the " *house.*" The former word is used of stations on a great road, where travellers found refreshment, so that here are the ideas of repose and progress. Further, Christ in *going* had in view His coming again.

SECOND DIALOGUE: THOMAS and JESUS (xiv. 5-7). *Thomas' Inquiry :* " Not knowing the goal, how can we know the way ? " *Jesus' Reply :* " The Father is the Goal, and I am the Way." Here the true Course, and Creed, and Character are brought to light: Christ the Way to Walk ; the Truth to Trust ; and the Life to Live. Truth, in the first place, is not something to *know*, but something to *be* ; it is not a dogma, but a life. Christ plainly declares His eternal oneness with the Father, that is, His own Deity (7).

THIRD DIALOGUE : PHILIP and JESUS (xiv. 8-21). *Philip's Inquiry*: " Shall we not be contented if Thou wilt shew us the Father ? " *Jesus' Reply*: " I am the revelation of the Father, and am ever with you, the power of life and of service." Verses 8-11, treat of the objective manifestation of God without the disciples: *their idea*. Verses 12–21, tell of the subjective manifestation of God within them; *Jesus' revelation*, With reference to the latter,— (a) By virtue of the disciples' relation to Christ, they will carry on His work after His departure (12–14). What are the "*greater works*"? Are they possible? Are you doing them?

Thought: HONEST DOUBT MAY BE THE PATH TO KNOWLEDGE.

ST. JOHN xiv. 15-31

Title: PROMISE AND PRECEPT

15 If ye love me, keep my commandments. 16 And I will pray the Father, and he shall give you another Comforter, that he may abide with you for ever; 17 Even the Spirit of truth; whom the world cannot receive, because it seeth him not, neither knoweth him: but ye know him; for he dwelleth with you, and shall be in you. 18 I will not leave you comfortless: I will come to you.

19 Yet a little while, and the world seeth me no more; but ye see me: because I live, ye shall live also. 20 At that day ye shall know that I am in my Father, and ye in me, and I in you. 21 He that hath my commandments, and keepeth them, he it is that loveth me: and he that loveth me shall be loved of my Father, and I will love him, and will manifest myself to him.

22 Judas saith unto him, not Iscariot, Lord, how is it that thou wilt manifest thyself unto us, and not unto the world?

23 Jesus answered and said unto him, If a man love me, he will keep my words: and my Father will love him, and we will come unto him, and make our abode with him. 24 He that loveth me not keepeth not my sayings: and the word which ye hear is not mine, but the Father's which sent me. 25 These things have I spoken unto you, being yet present with you. 26 But the Comforter, which is the Holy Ghost, whom the Father will send in my name, he shall teach you all things, and bring all things to your remembrance, whatsoever I have said unto you.

27 Peace I leave with you, my peace I give unto you : not as the world giveth, give I unto you. Let not your heart be troubled, neither let it be afraid. 28 Ye have heard how I said unto you, I go away, and come again unto you. If ye loved me, ye would rejoice, because I said, I go unto the Father : for my Father is greater than I. 29 And now I have told you before it come to pass, that, when it is come to pass, ye might believe. 30 Hereafter, I will not talk much with you : for the prince of this world cometh, and hath nothing in me. 31 But that the world may know that I love the Father ; and as the Father gave me commandment, even so I do.

Arise, let us go hence.

EXPOSITION

We here continue the subject of the preceding portion.

(b) Christ is about to leave His disciples, but He will make provision for them during His absence (15–17). Ponder carefully these great words. Mark two things. First, the *Trinity* in verse 16. "*I*" "*the Father*," "*Comforter*." As otherwise, Christ, without hesitation, associates Himself with the Father and the Spirit in a way that can only mean that He too is God. Incidentally here is evidence of the Personality of the Spirit.

Second, observe what is said about the Spirit, not only in verse 17, but throughout these chapters (xiv-xvi). Distinguish " *with*," and " *in* " in verse 17 : " *with* " characterises the previous dispensation ; and " *in* " the present age.

(c) The Master promises to come back to His own (18–21). The R.V. has rightly, " *I come to you* " as also in verse 3. This means, not only the Second Advent, but also in resurrection days, at Pentecost, and at other times. He teaches the disciples that *obedience* is the true expression of *love*.

Now comes, THE FOURTH DIALOGUE : JUDE and JESUS (xiv. 22-31). *Jude's Inquiry* : " What is the principle of Thy self-revelation ? " *Jesus' Reply* : The conditions, mode, and promise of that revelation are detailed. There are here three paragraphs (22–24).

Christ emphasises the truth just approached (21) that in order to receive divine communications men must both love and obey (25–27). He then fore-intimates the New Testament; the GOSPELS, "*will call all things to your remembrance*"; the EPISTLES, "*teach you all things*"; and the APOCALYPSE, "*things to come*" (xvi. 13); and He promises to His disciples His abiding *peace* (28–31). Once more Christ tells of His coming departure, and the effect of it. A closing word—"let us go hence" (31). As He goes with us, we need not fear to go.

Thought: *WE ARE NOT ORPHANS* (18 R.V. margin).

ST. JOHN xv. 1-17

Title: *FRUITFULNESS AND FRIENDSHIP*

1 I am the true vine, and my Father is the husbandman. 2 Every branch in me that beareth not fruit he taketh away: and every branch that beareth fruit, he purgeth it, that it may bring forth more fruit. 3 Now ye are clean through the word which I have spoken unto you.

4 Abide in me, and I in you. As the branch cannot bear fruit of itself, except it abide in the vine; no more can ye, except ye abide in me. 5 I am the vine, ye are the branches: He that abideth in me, and I in him, the same bringeth forth much fruit: for without me ye can do nothing. 6 If a man abide not in me, he is cast forth as a branch, and is withered; and men gather them, and cast them into the fire, and they are burned. 7 If ye abide in me, and my words abide in you, ye shall ask what ye will, and it shall be done unto you. 8 Herein is my Father glorified, that ye bear much fruit; so shall ye be my disciples.

9 As the Father hath loved me, so have I loved you: continue ye in my love. 10 If ye keep my commandments, ye shall abide in my love; even as I have kept my Father's commandments, and abide in his love. 11 These things have I spoken unto you, that my joy might remain in you, and that your joy might be full.

12 This is my commandment, That ye love one

another, as I have loved you. 13 Greater love hath no man than this, that a man lay down his life for his friends. 14 Ye are my friends, if ye do whatsoever I command you. 15 Henceforth I call you not servants ; for the servant knoweth not what his lord doeth : but I have called you friends ; for all things that I have heard of my Father I have made known unto you. 16 Ye have not chosen me, but I have chosen you, and ordained you, that ye should go and bring forth fruit, and that your fruit should remain : that whatsoever ye shall ask of the Father in my name, he may give it you. 17 These things I command you, that ye love one another.

EXPOSITION

There is inestimable treasure in these few verses. What multitudes have drunk at this crystal spring ! Our portion is in two parts : 1. *Life and Fruitfulness* (1–8), and 2. *Love and Friendship* (9–16).

LIFE AND FRUITFULNESS. Two things are assumed ; first, that there can be no fruitfulness where there is no life ; and second, that where there is life there is always some measure of fruitfulness. To these should be added the further thought that fruitfulness has reference, not to service, but to *character*. "But the fruit of the Spirit is love, joy, peace, longsuffering, gentleness, goodness, faith, meekness, temperance : against such there is no law." (Galatians v. 22, 23).

We are taught also that there are *degrees* of fruitfulness ; "*fruit*," "*more fruit*," "*much fruit*" (2, 5), or, according to the Synoptists, "thirtyfold, sixtyfold, and hundredfold." How much fruit are you bearing ? that is, how like Christ are you becoming ?

The victorious life is one, not of struggle, but of rest ; it is an *abiding*. The branch does not struggle to abide in the vine, but being vitally related to it, it just abides, partaking of the nourishment of the root, and without a struggle brings forth fruit. Is that your experience ?

LOVE AND FRIENDSHIP. Here is an entirely new ethic ! Friendship with Christ and fellowship with Christians are conditioned upon obedience to a command—*to love*. Only in the realm of things divine is *love a duty*. We may be God's *children* without being His *friends*; the one is based on His gift of life to us; the other, upon our offering of love to Him. Are you *a friend of God*?

You cannot have God and the World for friends at the same time.

"*The friendship of the world is enmity with God.*" The world hated and hates Christ, and therefore will not love you if you are like Him. Do you believe this?

Mark in our portion Christ's teaching on *Prayer*, verses 7, 16. Here is an unlimited promise resting on a limited condition.

Thought: TO LOVE IS TO LIVE.

ST. JOHN xv. 18-27

Title: THE CHURCH IN THE WORLD

18 If the world hate you, ye know that it hated me before it hated you. 19 If ye were of the world, the world would love his own: but because ye are not of the world, but I have chosen you out of the world, therefore the world hateth you. 20 Remember the word that I said unto you, The servant is not greater than his lord. If they have persecuted me, they will also persecute you; if they have kept my saying, they will keep your's also. 21 But all these things will they do unto you for my name's sake, because they know not him that sent me.

22 If I had not come and spoken unto them, they had not had sin: but now they have no cloke for their sin. 23 He that hateth me hateth my Father also. 24 If I had not done among them the works which none other man did, they had not had sin: but now have they both seen and hated both me and my Father. 25 But this cometh to pass, that the word might be fulfilled that is written in their law, They hated me without a cause.

26 But when the Comforter is come, whom I will send unto you from the Father, even the Spirit of truth, which proceedeth from the Father, he shall testify of me: 27 And ye also shall bear witness, because ye have been with me from the beginning.

EXPOSITION

If in verses 1-11 the subject is *The Disciples and Christ*, and in 12-17 *The Disciples and One Another*, in 18-27 it is *The Disciples' and the World*; and here we learn of the world's hatred, and the disciples, witness.

1. THE HATRED OF THE WORLD TOWARD THE DISCIPLES (18-25). The keynote here is, "*the servant is not greater than his Lord.*" Upon a time, at a social function, a lady expressed the opinion that if Jesus came to London to-day He would not be treated as He was in Jerusalem, but enthusiastically welcomed, and she appealed to Thomas Carlyle for endorsement of her view; whereupon that sage rasped out, "No, madam, if Christ came to London to-day they would take Him to Newgate and hang Him."

With all the changes which have taken place during the last 1900 years, *human nature has not changed*; its attitude towards God in Christ is fundamentally the same, though varied in its expression. The expression may change from violence to contempt, from contempt to respect, and from respect to indifference, but the principle remains the same.

2. THE WITNESS OF THE DISCIPLES TO THE WORLD (26-27); The disciples' declaration (27) follows the Spirit's instruction (26). The Christian's witness can be powerful only as it is informed and inspired: mark both these things, and not only the latter. It is to CHRIST and of Him that both the Spirit and the disciples bear witness. To speak rightly and effectively of Him it is necessary that we be "*with Him*" (27), and so, know Him.

Remember, it is not *gramophones* that are wanted, but *voices*. This is a chapter full of sharp contrasts, a feature characteristic of the Apostle John's Writings. He draws a clear line of distinction between light and darkness, life and death, right and wrong, Church and World, truth and error, God and Satan. Do you think clearly?

The *hate* of which Christ so often speaks is not necessarily, as often, a feeling of personal animosity, but an attitude of soul to His claims. When, in another place (Luke xiv. 26), He makes *hating* a condition of discipleship, He means that no one and nothing must be preferred to Him. As the world prefers itself to Him, it is said to *hate* Him.

Thought : BE TRUE TO CHRIST IN A SINFUL WORLD.

ST. JOHN xvi. 1-15

Title : THE SPIRIT IN THE WORLD, AND IN THE CHURCH

1 These things have I spoken unto you, that ye should not be offended. 2 They shall put you out of the synagogues ; yea, the time cometh, that whosoever killeth you will think that he doeth God service. 3 And these things will they do unto you, because they have not known the Father, nor me. 4a But these things have I told you, that when the time shall come, ye may remember that I told you of them.

4b And these things I said not unto you at the beginning, because I was with you. 5 But now I go my way to him that sent me ; and none of you asketh me, Whither goest thou ? 6 But because I have said these things unto you, sorrow hath filled your heart.

7 Nevertheless I tell you the truth : It is expedient for you that I go away : for if I go not away, the Comforter will not come unto you ; but if I depart, I will send him unto you. 8 And when he is come, he will reprove the world of sin, and of righteousness, and of judgment : 9 Of sin, because they believe not on me ; 10 Of righteousness, because I go to my Father, and ye see me no more ; 11 Of judgment, because the prince of this world is judged. 12 I have yet many things to say unto you, but ye cannot bear them now.

13 Howbeit when he, the Spirit of truth, is come, he will guide you into all truth : for he shall not speak of himself ; but whatsoever he shall hear, that shall he speak ; and he will shew you things to come. 14 He shall glorify me : for he shall receive of mine, and shall shew it unto you. 15 All things that the Father hath are mine : therefore

said I, that he shall take of mine, and shall shew it unto you.

EXPOSITION

1. THE SPIRIT AND THE WORLD (1-11). In chapter xv. 18-25, we read of the hatred of the world. Here, in verses 1-4a, the subject is continued, and we are shown that its activity is the expression of a false religious zeal. Fancy people ignorant of the Father and the Son imagining that they can "*do God service!*" Perhaps the outstanding illustration of this is Saul of Tarsus; but still there are numberless people who "have a zeal, but not according to knowledge." The most difficult *world* to deal with, is the *religious* world.

The Lord now tells the disciples that the mission of the Spirit is conditioned upon His own departure from them (4b-7). It is worth while to mark the Master's reasons for not having before said certain things (4), and for now saying them (1, ch. xiv. 29). His teaching was and is according to the capacity of His disciples to apprehend (12); and this is a fundamental principle of all teaching.

When Jesus ascended, His local presence gave way to His universal presence. That necessity made His departure *expedient* (7). We have not lost but gained by His going from the world, as to bodily presence.

In verses 8-11 is detailed the Spirit's mission in the world (a wonderful paragraph). The text is verse 8, and the exposition of it is in verses 9-11. These are the three great things—Sin, Righteousness, Judgment, and mark, judgment *past*, not to come.

The second passage is on, 2. THE SPIRIT AND THE CHURCH (12-15). These verses anticipate not only a *revelation*, but also a *record*. "The same trust which leads us to believe that the Apostles were guided into the Truth, leads us also to believe that by the providential leading of the Spirit they were so guided as to present it in such a way that it might remain in a permanent form" (Westcott).

Thought: *WHAT A COMFORT TO HAVE THE THE COMFORTER.*

ST. JOHN xvi. 16-33

Title: LAST WORDS

16 A little while, and ye shall not see me : and again, a little while, and ye shall see me, because I go to the Father.

17 Then said some of his disciples among themselves, What is this that he saith unto us, A little while, and ye shall not see me : and again, A little while, and ye shall see me : and, Because I go to to the Father ? 18 They said therefore, What is this that he saith, A little while ? we cannot tell what he saith.

19 Now Jesus knew that they were desirous to ask him, and said unto them, Do ye enquire among yourselves of that I said, A little while, and ye shall not see me : and again, A little while, and ye shall see me ?

20 Verily, verily, I say unto you, That ye shall weep and lament, but the world shall rejoice : and ye shall be sorrowful, but your sorrow shall be turned into joy. 21 A woman when she is in travail hath sorrow, because her hour is come : but as soon as she is delivered of the child, she remembereth no more the anguish, for joy that a man is born into the world. 22 And ye now therefore have sorrow : but I will see you again and your heart shall rejoice, and your joy no man taketh from you.

23 And in that day ye shall ask me nothing. Verily, verily, I say unto you, Whatsoever ye shall ask the Father in my name, he will give it you. 24 Hitherto have ye asked nothing in my name : ask, and ye shall receive, that your joy may be full. 25 These things have I spoken unto you in proverbs : but the time cometh, when I shall no more speak unto you in proverbs, but I shall shew you plainly of the Father.

26 At that day ye shall ask in my name : and I say not unto you, that I will pray the Father for you : 27 For the Father himself loveth you, because ye have loved me, and have believed that I came out from God. 28 I came forth from the Father, and am come into the world : again, I leave the world, and go to the Father.

29 His disciples said unto him, Lo, now speakest thou plainly, and speakest no proverb. 30 Now

are we sure that thou knowest all things, and needest not that any man should ask thee : by this we believe that thou camest forth from God.

31 Jesus answered them, Do ye now believe ? 32 Behold, the hour cometh, yea, is now come, that ye shall be scattered, every man to his own, and shall leave me alone : and yet I am not alone, because the Father is with me. 33 These things I have spoken unto you, that in me ye might have peace. In the world ye shall have tribulation : but be of good cheer ; I have overcome the world.

EXPOSITION

There now draws to a close the Lord's last discourse to the inner circle of His disciples. He tells them that when He departs they will stand in quite *a new relation* to Him, and this puzzled them (16–18). He further tells them that before them is a time of *sorrow*, to be followed by *joy*, the joy to come out of the sorrow (19–22). Nowhere are Christians led to expect immunity from sorrow in this world ; but neither does the New Testament teach that sorrow and joy are mutually exclusive ; that at any given time we have either the one or the other. On the contrary it teaches that *joy is transfigured sorrow* (20) ; that neither can exist without the other.

It was in this week of Christ's most poignant sorrow that He talked most about His joy. Have you noticed that ? Mark His references to *joy* in these two last discourses. The Apostle Paul had caught His Master's meaning when he said, " *sorrowful yet always rejoicing.*"

Next, Jesus speaks to His Apostles about *the future* (23–28). " *The day* " referred to in verse 23 began at Pentecost, and will close when Christ returns ; it has lasted already nearly 2,000 years. Mark the two words (*erōtēsete*, and *aitēsēte*) translated " ask " in verse 23. " *Ye shall ask me nothing,*" means, that there would no longer be any need *to ask Him any questions* ; verse 19 shows this, where the same word is used. But, " whatsoever ye shall *ask* the Father," refers to *prayer*. After a *confession* from the disciples (29-30) Jesus speaks a final word of warning and assurance (31-33). Think of it! in the deep shadow of the Cross, He says to this handful of men, " CHEER UP, I HAVE CONQUERED." There is nothing to compare with this in all history. Have you cheered up ? Are you living in His victory ?

Thought : *BY FAITH TRANSMUTE YOUR SORROW INTO JOY.*

ST. JOHN xvii. 1-12

Title : INTERCESSION

1 These words spake Jesus, and lifted up his eyes to heaven, and said, Father, the hour is come ; glorify thy Son, that thy Son also may glorify thee : 2 As thou hast given him power over all flesh, that he should give eternal life to as many as thou hast given him. 3 And this is life eternal, that they might know thee the only true God, and Jesus Christ, whom thou hast sent. 4 I have glorified thee on the earth : I have finished the work which thou gavest me to do. 5 And now, O Father, glorify thou me with thine own self with the glory which I had with thee before the world was.

6 I have manifested thy name unto the men which thou gavest me out of the world : thine they were, and thou gavest them me ; and they have kept thy word. 7 Now they have known that all things whatsoever thou hast given me are of thee. 8 For I have given unto them the words which thou gavest me ; and they have received them, and have known surely that I came out from thee, and they have believed that thou didst send me.

9 I pray for them : I pray not for the world, but for them which thou hast given me ; for they are thine. 10 And all mine are thine, and thine are mine ; and I am glorified in them. 11 And now I am no more in the world, but these are in the world, and I come to thee. Holy Father, keep through thine own name those whom thou hast given me, that they may be one, as we are. 12 While I was with them in the world, I kept them in thy name : those thou gavest me I have kept, and none of them is lost, but the son of perdition ; that the scripture might be fulfilled.

EXPOSITION

Relative to the disciples, in xiii. 1-30, we have INTRODUCTION OF THE LIGHT TO THEM: in xiii. 31 to xvi. 33, IMPARTATION OF THE LIGHT TO THEM; and now, in xvii, INTERCESSION FOR THE LIGHT IN THEM. It would not be seemly to attempt too acute an analysis of any true prayer, least of all of this one. The out-pouring of the soul of the Redeemer is for our worshipful contemplation rather than for critical analysis. Nevertheless, we may discern here certain movements of thought.

Having regard for the *subjects* of the prayer, observe. 1. CHRIST'S PRAYER FOR HIMSELF (1-5). 2. CHRIST'S PRAYER FOR HIS DISCIPLES (6-19). 3. CHRIST'S PRAYER FOR THE WHOLE CHURCH (20-26).

And having regard for the *substance* of the Prayer, mark these great notes: (a) *Revelation* (1-5); (b) *Preservation* (6-16). (c) *Sanctification* (17-19). (d) *Unification* (20-23). (e) *Glorification* (24-26).

The *Revelation* of the past and future glory of the redeeming Son makes possible the individual *Preservation* and *Sanctification* of those whom He has redeemed. These individual blessings enjoyed would find expression in spiritual *Unity* throughout the whole Church, and this will issue finally in the *Glorification* of all who have been so divinely enlightened and loved.

This is the LORD'S PRAYER: that in Matthew vi, is the DISCIPLES' PRAYER. Trace these dominating words in this Prayer: *Father, Glorify, Kept, Word, Pray, Even as* (so), *Sent, One, Know, Name, Loved.*

Observe in this Prayer the clear-cut distinction which is made between the *Church* and the *World*; and between *believers* and *unbelievers*. Love is essentially self-forgetful and sacrificial, and so *giving* is a dominating note throughout. There is much talk to-day about *Church Union*. What is of vastly greater importance is *Christian Unity*. Is Christ's prayer being answered in you?

Thought: THE SENT ONE HAS SENT ME (18).

ST. JOHN xvii. 13-26

Title : WHAT CHRIST ASKS FOR US

13 And now come I to thee ; and these things I speak in the world, that they might have my joy fulfilled in themselves. 14 I have given them thy word ; and the world hath hated them, because they are not of the world, even as I am not of the world. 15 I pray not that thou shouldest take them out of the world, but that thou shouldest keep them from the evil. 16 They are not of the world, even as I am not of the world.

17 Sanctify them through thy truth : thy word is truth. 18 As thou hast sent me into the world, even so have I also sent them into the world. 19 And for their sakes I sanctify myself, that they also might be sanctified through the truth.

20 Neither pray I for these alone, but for them also which shall believe on me through their word ; 21 That they all may be one ; as thou, Father, art in me, and I in thee, that they also may be one in us : that the world may believe that thou hast sent me.

22 And the glory which thou gavest me I have given them ; that they may be one, even as we are one : 23 I in them, and thou in me, that they may be made perfect in one ; and that the world may know that thou hast sent me, and hast loved them, as thou hast loved me.

24 Father, I will that they also, whom thou hast given me, be with me where I am ; that they may behold my glory, which thou hast given me : for thou lovedst me before the foundation of the world.

25 O righteous Father, the world hath not known thee : but I have known thee, and these have known that thou hast sent me. 26 And I have declared unto them thy name, and will declare it : that the love wherewith thou hast loved me may be in them, and I in them.

EXPOSITION

We have looked at this momentous chapter in outline, but a thousand readings of it will not allow of our exhausting its spiritual treasures. Take its sentences and its dominating words one by one, and ponder them carefully and prayerfully. Surely in our hearts we often say,—" I want that the will of God shall be done in me, but how am I to know what God's will for me is ?" So far as our lesson is concerned we are not left in doubt, for what Christ asks the Father for us, must be His will for us. For what then, does He ask ?

1. It is God's will, first of all, that we be *saved* (2, 3); and then, that we be *kept* (11). Christ prays not for our removal from the world, but for our moral and spiritual safety in it (15).

2. Further, it is God's will that we be *sanctified* (17, 19). It is not enough that we be safeguarded: " this is the will of God, even your sanctification." Sanctification is separation, separation is by holiness, and holiness is spiritual health.

3. It is God's will that we be *witnesses* (20) in order that others may be saved. How can people believe if they do not hear, and how can they hear without a preacher ? Every saved soul should be a preacher.

4. For this purpose, it is God's will that we all become *missionaries* (18), that is, *sent ones*. It does not say *how far* anyone will be sent. If you go to perishing souls in your own city or village you are a missionary. But, obviously, many must go far afield.

5. Again, it is God's will that *unity* should characterize His Church (22, 23). Christian Unity, which only God Himself can create, we must *keep* (Eph. iv. 3).

6. Once more, it is God's will that we should *love* one another, as He has loved us (26). Christ's love for us is to be the standard, though it cannot be the measure, of our love for one another. How amazing a possibility ! How tragic is our failure !

7. And finally, it is God's will that we spend a blissful eternity with Him in heaven (24, xiv. 1–4). Is the risen Lord's prayer for *you* being answered in your experience ? There is power in His prayer: but is there purpose in your heart ?

Thought : GOD'S WILL IS OUR PEACE.

ST. JOHN xviii. 1-14

Title: THE BETRAYAL

1 When Jesus had spoken these words, he went forth with his disciples over the brook Cedron, where was a garden, into the which he entered, and his disciples. 2 And Judas also, which betrayed him, knew the place; for Jesus ofttimes resorted thither with his disciples. 3 Judas then, having received a band of men and officers from the chief priests and Pharisees, cometh thither with lanterns and torches and weapons.

4 Jesus therefore, knowing all things that should come upon him, went forth, and said unto them, Whom seek ye? 5 They answered him, Jesus of Nazareth. Jesus saith unto them, I am he. And Judas also, which betrayed him, stood with them. 6 As soon then as he had said unto them, I am he, they went backward, and fell to the ground.

7 Then asked he them again, Whom seek ye? And they said, Jesus of Nazareth. 8 Jesus answered, I have told you that I am he: if therefore ye seek me, let these go their way: 9 That the saying might be fulfilled, which he spake, Of them which thou gavest me have I lost none.

10 Then Simon Peter having a sword drew it, and smote the high priest's servant, and cut off his right ear. The servant's name was Malchus. 11 Then said Jesus unto Peter, Put up thy sword into the sheath: the cup which my Father hath given me, shall I not drink it?

12 Then the band and the captain and officers of the Jews took Jesus, and bound him, 13 And led him away to Annas first: for he was father in law to Caiaphas, which was the high priest that same year. 14 Now Caiaphas was he, which gave counsel to the Jews, that it was expedient that one man should die for the people.

EXPOSITION

We must pause here again to get the perspective of this " Gospel." It is in three main divisions, with a *Prologue* (i. 1–18), and *Epilogue* (xxi). They are: I. THE REVELATION OF THE SON TO THE WORLD AS LIFE (i. 19–xii. 50). II. THE REVELATION OF THE SON TO THE DISCIPLES AS LIGHT (xiii–xvii). And now we come to III. THE REVELATION OF THE SON TO THE DISCIPLES AND THE WORLD AS LOVE (xviii–xx). Put these divisions in your Bible margin. The last division is in three parts, the *Trial*, the *Tragedy*, and the *Triumph of Divine Love*.

First of all then, 1. THE TRIAL OF DIVINE LOVE (xviii. 1–xix. 16). Verses 12–14, belong to the next portion, so we shall not now consider them. This lesson records *The Betrayal* (1–11). Things specially noteworthy in this portion are :—

(a) That Gethsemane was a place often frequented by Jesus and His disciples (1, 2). Take time to let that impress you ;

(b) That Jesus knew all that was to happen to Him (4). Modern teaching which affirms his fallibility denies that He foreknew.

(c) That thrice here, Jesus said " I AM " (5, 6, 8) He had said that before, and Judas at any rate must have discerned the deeper meaning of this reply (cf. iv. 26 ; vi. 20 ; viii. 24, 28, 58 ; xiii. 19).

(d) That Peter, as often before, showed more courage than sense on this occasion (10). That he was not arrested can be accounted for only by the fact that Jesus healed Malchus' ear (Luke).

(e) That one who had companied with Jesus for two years at least, had heard His wonderful words, seen His wonderful deeds, and beheld His wonderful life, now betrayed Him ! (2). Judas must for ever remain a mystery : he did what can never be repeated, but it is in the power and choice of each of us in some other way to betray Christ. Are you doing this by your refusal to bear witness to Him ? By your love of the world ? By your neglect of His Word and prayer ? In any other way ?

Thought : HAVE I MORAL KINSHIP WITH JUDAS?

ST. JOHN xviii. 15-27

Title : PLAYING WITH JUSTICE

15 And Simon Peter followed Jesus, and so did another disciple : that disciple was known unto the

high priest, and went in with Jesus into the palace of the high priest. 16 But Peter stood at the door without. Then went out that other disciple, which was known unto the high priest, and spake unto her that kept the door, and brought in Peter. 17 Then saith the damsel that kept the door unto Peter, Art not thou also one of this man's disciples? He saith, I am not. 18 And the servants and officers stood there, who had made a fire of coals; for it was cold: and they warmed themselves: and Peter stood with them, and warmed himself.

19 The high priest then asked Jesus of his disciples, and of his doctrine. 20 Jesus answered him, I spake openly to the world; I ever taught in the synagogue, and in the temple, whither the Jews always resort; and in secret have I said nothing. 21 Why askest thou me? ask them which heard me, what I have said unto them: behold, they know what I said.

22 And when he had thus spoken, one of the officers which stood by struck Jesus with the palm of his hand, saying, Answerest thou the high priest so? 23 Jesus answered him, If I have spoken evil, bear witness of the evil: but if well, why smitest thou me?

24 Now Annas had sent him bound unto Caiaphas the high priest.

25 And Simon Peter stood and warmed himself. They said therefore unto him, Art not thou also one of his disciples? He denied it, and said, I am not. 26 One of the servants of the high priest, being his kinsman whose ear Peter cut off, saith, Did not I see thee in the garden with him? 27 Peter then denied again: and immediately the cock crew.

EXPOSITION

Following *The Betrayal* (1-11) are *The Trials* (xviii. 12 to xix. 16); and first of all:—

1. THE ECCLESIASTICAL TRIAL (12-27). This was first before ANNAS (13), and then before CAIAPHAS (24). Part of this report is peculiar to the Fourth Gospel. Observe that of these sixteen verses, seven are not about the trial of *Jesus*, but of *Peter* (15-18, 25-27). Look at this first. Every one who names the Name of Christ is on his trial. If the Master was

arraigned it is not likely that the servant will escape. Now, where did Peter begin to go wrong ? In wishing it to be thought that he had nothing to do with Jesus. Have you ever felt like that in worldly company ? That is how we are likely to feel when we *voluntarily* go into worldly company.

Courage and cowardice strangely mingled in Peter. He could draw a sword at the Garden gate, and relieve a man of his ear, and yet in this courtyard he denied his Lord before a giggling girl. Watch yourself on *occasions*. An assumed boldness is ever a characteristic of fear. Peter's tongue followed his feet, and as they were astray, it was atheistic. God does not promise to protect us in places where we should not be.

Now look at the other trial (12-14, 19-24). How different ! Christ was led away by His captors, not because He was helpless, but because He was willing : it was not their fetters which bound Him, but His love. They asked Him of His doctrine and disciples, not to believe, but in order to incriminate. Are your enquiries always honest ?

Jesus pointed them to His public teaching (20-21). He had not been a schemer behind locked doors, but a preacher out in the open. These religious humbugs found it easier to strike Christ than to convict Him (22) : so do their large posterity.

Never was justice more grossly perverted than in these so-called *trials* of Jesus.

Thought : BETTER DIE FOR YOUR LORD THAN DENY HIM.

ST. JOHN xviii. 28-40

Title : A JUDGE ASKS THE PROSECUTION FOR ADVICE !

28 Then led they Jesus from Caiaphas unto the hall of judgment : and it was early ; and they themselves went not into the judgment hall, lest they should be defiled ; but that they might eat the passover. 29 Pilate then went out unto them, and said, What accusation bring ye against this man ?

30 They answered and said unto him, If he were not a malefactor, we would not have delivered him up unto thee.

31 Then said Pilate unto them, Take ye him, and judge him according to your law. The Jews therefore said unto him, It is not lawful for us to put any man to death : 32 That the saying of Jesus might be fulfilled, which he spake, signifying what death he should die.

33 Then Pilate entered into the judgment hall again, and called Jesus, and said unto him, Art thou the King of the Jews ?

34 Jesus answered him, Sayest thou this thing of thyself, or did others tell it thee of me ?

35 Pilate answered, Am I a Jew ? Thine own nation and the chief priests have delivered thee unto me : what hast thou done ?

36 Jesus answered, My kingdom is not of this world : if my kingdom were of this world, then would my servants fight, that I should not be delivered to the Jews ; but now is my kingdom not from hence.

37 Pilate therefore said unto him, Art thou a king then ?

Jesus answered, Thou sayest that I am a king. To this end was I born, and for this cause came I into the world, that I should bear witness unto the truth. Every one that is of the truth heareth my voice.

38 Pilate saith unto him, What is truth ?

And when he had said this, he went out again unto the Jews, and saith unto them, I find in him no fault at all. 39 But ye have a custom, that I should release unto you one at the passover : will ye therefore that I release unto you the King of the Jews ?

40 Then cried they all again, saying, Not this man, but Barabbas. Now Barabbas was a robber.

EXPOSITION

2. THE CIVIL TRIAL (xviii. 28 to xix. 16). The scene of this Trial moves to and fro in relation to the Prætorium (28), now being without, and now within. Mark these movements : *without* (28–32) ; *within* (33–38a) ; *without* (38b–40) ; *within* (xix. 1–3) ; *without* (xix. 4–7) ; *within* (xix. 8–11) ; and finally

without (xix. 12–16). Three of these seven sections claim our attention now.

(i) First of all we hear Pilate asking the Jews what the charge is (28–32). It is clear that the Jews wanted nothing less than a death sentence, and the pronouncement of that was not in their power (31). How do man's malignity and God's mercy dovetail ! (32, cf. xii. 32). Two facts must ever be seen together, namely, that Jesus was put to death by men, and that He died voluntarily.

(ii) In the second section (33–38a), which is peculiar to this Record, Pilate has a private interview with Jesus. Who in this scene is the real King ? Then, Jesus stood before Pilate ; one day Pilate will stand before Jesus. *God* stood before a *governor*! Of course Pilate did not know this, but it was his business to be just. The *truth* must prevail (37). Christ Who was the Truth, was born to bear witness to it. Do you know to what end *you* were born ? and for what cause *you* came into the world ? (37). Human life is a plan of God, and every one must either *frustrate* or *fulfil* that plan. What are you doing ?

" God has a life plan for every human person, girding him visibly, or invisibly, for some exact thing, which it will be the chief significance and glory of his life to have accomplished " (*Bushnell*).

(iii) The third section (38b–40) shows us what a mockery Pilate's justice was. " *I find in him no fault, but—*" He used a *custom* (39) as a sop to his conscience. The choice is between *a robber* and the *Redeemer*, and the people do not hesitate (40). What *Barabbas* are you choosing instead of Christ ? Remember, there is always an alternative, but it is always fatal.

Thought : *LET YOUR KNOWLEDGE OF CHRIST BE FIRST HAND* (33, 34).

ST. JOHN xix. 1-16

Title : *THE CRUELTY OF HATE*

1 Then Pilate therefore took Jesus, and scourged him. 2 And the soldiers platted a crown of thorns,

and put it on his head, and they put on him a purple robe, 3 And said, Hail, King of the Jews! and they smote him with their hands.

4 Pilate therefore went forth again, and saith unto them, Behold, I bring him forth to you, that ye may know that I find no fault in him.

5 Then came Jesus forth, wearing the crown of thorns, and the purple robe.

And Pilate saith unto them, Behold the man!

6 When the chief priests therefore and officers saw him, they cried out, saying, Crucify him, crucify him. Pilate saith unto them, Take ye him, and crucify him: for I find no fault in him.

7 The Jews answered him, We have a law, and by our law he ought to die, because he made himself the Son of God.

8 When Pilate therefore heard that saying, he was the more afraid; 9 And went again into the judgment hall, and saith unto Jesus, Whence art thou?

But Jesus gave him no answer.

10 Then saith Pilate unto him, Speakest thou not unto me? knowest thou not that I have power to crucify thee, and have power to release thee?

11 Jesus answered, Thou couldest have no power at all against me, except it were given thee from above: therefore he that delivered me unto thee hath the greater sin.

12 And from thenceforth Pilate sought to release him: but the Jews cried out, saying, If thou let this man go, thou art not Cæsar's friend: whosoever maketh himself a king speaketh against Cæsar.

13 When Pilate therefore heard that saying, he brought Jesus forth, and sat down in the judgment seat in a place that is called the Pavement, but in the Hebrew, Gabbatha. 14 And it was the preparation of the passover, and about the sixth hour: and he saith unto the Jews, Behold your King!

15 But they cried out, Away with him, crucify him. Pilate saith unto them, Shall I crucify your King? The chief priests answered, We have no king but Cæsar. 16 Then delivered he him therefore unto them to be crucified. And they took Jesus, and led him away.

EXPOSITION

For the connection see the preceding portion.

(iv) The judge is fast becoming the criminal (1–3). Why was Jesus scourged ? Why was a crown of thorns put on His brow ? Why was He smitten ? Why was He mocked ? *Why?* It is clear that Pilate allowed all this in the hope that it would satisfy the Jews, and that in this way Jesus would escape the cross (Luke xxiii. 22).

But no motive can make wrong right; we may never do evil that good may come. If Jesus was not guilty He should not have been punished. When a judge sacrifices the claims of justice to the clamour of the crowd, he has pronounced his own sentence.

(v) The previous outrage was inside the Prætorium; this one is outside, before the crowd (4–7). Pilate had tried to save Jesus by *cruelty*; now he would save Him by an appeal to *pity* (5). Three times he declared that he *found no fault* in the prisoner; his duty then was obvious, he should have pronounced Him "not guilty," and have released Him. Are you playing tricks with your conscience ? Christ does not want pity, but fair play. What is to be said about such a verdict as this—"*take ye him, and crucify, for I find no fault in him*"? Pilate had said, "*ye have a custom*" (xviii. 39); and now the Jews say, "*we have a law*" (7). Yes, in the name of custom, law, and of every order and institution, get Truth out of the way; that has been the age-long impulse of the world.

(vi) Pilate has another private interview with Jesus (8–11). In the first (xviii. 33–38a), he talked about *Kingship*; now he chatters about *power*. Power, indeed ! Pilate seems to have had little of that.

(vii) The Governor, who had utter contempt for the Jews, now taunts them (14, 15), but all is at Jesus' expense (12–16). Pilate handed Him over, and they led Him away (16). Is not that a horrible farce ?

Thought : NEVER TRIFLE WITH THE TRUTH.

ST. JOHN xix. 17-30

Title : THE SAVIOUR DIES

17 And he bearing his cross went forth into a place called the place of a skull, which is called in the Hebrew Golgotha: 18 Where they crucified him, and two other with him, on either side one, and Jesus in the midst.

19 And Pilate wrote a title, and put it on the cross. And the writing was, JESUS OF NAZARETH THE KING OF THE JEWS. 20 This title then read many of the Jews : for the place where Jesus was crucified was nigh to the city : and it was written in Hebrew, and Greek, and Latin. 21 Then said the chief priests of the Jews to Pilate, Write not, The King of the Jews ; but that he said, I am King of the Jews. 22 Pilate answered, What I have written I have written.

23 Then the soldiers, when they had crucified Jesus, took his garments, and made four parts, to every soldier a part ; and also his coat : now the coat was without seam, woven from the top throughout. 24 They said therefore among themselves, Let us not rend it, but cast lots for it, whose it shall be : that the scripture might be fulfilled, which saith, They parted my raiment among them, and for my vesture they did cast lots. These things therefore the soldiers did.

25 Now there stood by the cross of Jesus his mother, and his mother's sister, Mary the wife of Cleophas, and Mary Magdalene. 26 When Jesus therefore saw his mother, and the disciple standing by, whom he loved, he saith unto his mother, Woman, behold thy son! 27 Then saith he to the disciple, Behold thy mother! And from that hour that disciple took her unto his own home.

28 After this, Jesus knowing that all things were now accomplished, that the scripture might be fulfilled, saith, I thirst. 29 Now there was set a vessel full of vinegar : and they filled a spunge with vinegar, and put it upon hyssop, and put it to his mouth. 30 When Jesus therefore had received the vinegar, he said, It is finished : and he bowed his head, and gave up the ghost.

EXPOSITION

In xviii. 1 to xix. 16, we have seen THE TRIAL OF DIVINE LOVE; now we are to behold THE TRAGEDY OF DIVINE LOVE (xix. 17–42).

> "Beneath an Eastern sky,
> Amid a rabble cry,
> A Man went forth to die,
>   FOR ME.
> Thorn-crowned His blessed head,
> Blood-stained His every tread,
> Cross-laden on He sped,
>   FOR ME!"

Do you believe that? If so, what difference does your belief make? Contemplate.

1. *The Crucifixion* (17–22). Jesus was and always is "*in the midst*" (18). Trace this fact and thought from the Cradle to the Throne. Though Jesus was alone in His death, He did not die alone (18). These men were so near, and yet so far. The title on the cross was written in the languages of Religion, Art and Law (20). How prophetic! Pilate became authoritative and firm too late (22). "*Too late*" are terrible words: you see to it that you are not too late.

2. *Foes and Friends* (23–27). Christ was never without both. How great the contrast here: cruelty and selfishness, on the one hand (23, 24); tenderness and self-forgetfulness, on the other hand (25–27). It will be eternally to the credit of these four women (three of them named Mary) that they stood by in this dark hour (25). Are not verses 26, 27, wonderful! This is the third of the SEVEN SAYINGS from the Cross. The veil is drawn, but we know how John would tenderly love and care for Mary. Trace the sentence in verse 26 five times.

3. *The Work Accomplished* (28–30). Here we have *Sayings* five and six. Will you think about them all to-day? "I THIRST." Is He thirsting still: thirsting for your love and witness; is He? "IT IS FINISHED." Read iv. 34; v. 36; xvii. 4; and xviii.

28. Christ did what He came to do. His death was not a surprise to Him, for He came to die. *Finished.* FINISHED. Hallelujah! What a Saviour!

Thought: *CHRIST IS THE FINISHER AS WELL AS THE AUTHOR OF FAITH* (Heb. xii. 2).

ST. JOHN xix. 31-42

Title: *GOD TAKES CARE OF JESUS' BODY*

31 The Jews therefore, because it was the preparation, that the bodies should not remain upon the cross on the sabbath day, (for that sabbath day was an high day,) besought Pilate that their legs might be broken, and that they might be taken away. 32 Then came the soldiers, and brake the legs of the first, and of the other which was crucified with him. 33 But when they came to Jesus, and saw that he was dead already, they brake not his legs: 34 But one of the soldiers with a spear pierced his side, and forthwith came there out blood and water.

35 And he that saw it bare record, and his record is true: and he knoweth that he saith true, that ye might believe. 36 For these things were done, that the scripture should be fulfilled, A bone of him shall not be broken. 37 And again another scripture saith, They shall look on him whom they pierced.

38 And after this Joseph of Arimathæa, being a disciple of Jesus, but secretly for fear of the Jews, besought Pilate that he might take away the body of Jesus: and Pilate gave him leave. He came therefore, and took the body of Jesus.

39 And there came also Nicodemus, which at the first came to Jesus by night, and brought a mixture of myrrh and aloes, about an hundred pound weight. 40 Then took they the body of Jesus, and wound it in linen clothes with the spices, as the manner of the Jews is to bury.

41 Now in the place where he was crucified there was a garden: and in the garden a new sepulchre, wherein was never man yet laid. 42 There laid they Jesus therefore because of the Jews' preparation day: for the sepulchre was nigh at hand.

EXPOSITION

Here are two requests :—

1. *The Request of the Jews* (31–37). This had important consequences, the fulfilment of two predictions. It had been foretold that " *a bone of Him shall not be broken* " (Exod. and Num.), and although the legs were broken, of the two malefactors, Jesus' were not. It had been predicted also that the Jews would look upon Him whom they had pierced (cf. Zech: xii. 10 ; Rev. i. 7), and this they now do.

Westcott thinks that the flow of " *blood and water* " is to be regarded " as a sign of life in death " : also, he sees in the " blood," a cleansing power, and in the " water," a quickening power ; the one referring specially to Christ's work, and the other, to the Spirit's work. It is worthy of note that the Evangelist says the first Scripture was then " *fulfilled* " (36), but his language regarding the second passage safeguards it for a future fulfilment (37). This is an evidence of inspiration.

2. *The Request of Joseph of Arimathæa* (38–42). In verse 25, we saw the devotion of women : here we see how devoted men can be. JOSEPH and NICODEMUS, both disciples of Christ, now lavish upon Him a love which He could have done with while He was alive ; but better late than not at all. The story of Nicodemus can be told in three sentences : (a) *Desire for Christ* (iii. 1–21) ; (b) *Defence of Christ* (vii. 45–52) ; and *Devotion to Christ* (39). Mark the progress.

A CROSS, a GARDEN, a TOMB, a BODY ! (41–42) : here ugliness and beauty, death and life meet ; but it is the beauty and the life that triumph. Jesus suffered all this for you. Do you love Him ? Have you thanked Him ? Are you living for Him ? Are you ?

Thought: I WILL NOT BE A SECRET DISCIPLE (38).

ST. JOHN xx. 1-18

Title : *THE RISEN LORD APPEARS*

1 The first day of the week cometh Mary Magdalene early, when it was yet dark, unto the sepulchre, and seeth the stone taken away from the sepulchre. 2 Then she runneth, and cometh to Simon Peter, and to the other disciple, whom Jesus loved, and saith unto them, They have taken away the Lord out of the sepulchre, and we know not where they have laid him. 3 Peter therefore went forth, and that other disciple, and came to the sepulchre. 4 So they ran both together : and the other disciple did outrun Peter, and came first to the sepulchre. 5 And he stooping down, and looking in, saw the linen clothes lying ; yet went he not in. 6 Then cometh Simon Peter following him, and went into the sepulchre, and seeth the linen clothes lie, 7 And the napkin, that was about his head, not lying with the linen clothes, but wrapped together in a place by itself. 8 Then went in also that other disciple, which came first to the sepulchre, and he saw, and believed. 9 For as yet they knew not the scripture, that he must rise again from the dead. 10 Then the disciples went away again unto their own home.

11 But Mary stood without at the sepulchre weeping : and as she wept, she stooped down, and looked into the sepulchre, 12 And seeth two angels in white sitting, the one at the head, and the other at the feet, where the body of Jesus had lain. 13 And they say unto her, Woman, why weepest thou ? She saith unto them, Because they have taken away my Lord, and I know not where they have laid him. 14 And when she had thus said, she turned herself back, and saw Jesus standing, and knew not that it was Jesus.

15 Jesus saith unto her, Woman, why weepest thou ? whom seekest thou ?

She, supposing him to be the gardener, saith unto him, Sir, if thou have borne him hence, tell me where thou hast laid him, and I will take him away.

16 Jesus saith unto her, Mary.

She turned herself, and saith unto him, Rabboni ; which is to say, Master.

17 Jesus saith unto her, Touch me not ; for I am

not yet ascended to my Father: but go to my brethren, and say unto them, I ascend unto my Father, and your Father; and to my God, and your God.

18 Mary Magdalene came and told the disciples that she had seen the Lord, and that he had spoken these things unto her.

EXPOSITION

We now come to the closing scenes of this wonderful record: THE TRIUMPH OF DIVINE LOVE. In this chapter we find *a Twofold Preparation for a Threefold Revelation*.

Look first at THE PREPARATION (1–10). The people prepared for the new revelation of Christ are MARY MAGDALENE, PETER, and JOHN the Apostle; and the signs by which they are prepared are, the open sepulchre, and the folded grave-clothes. Mary sees the first of these signs, and the men see the other two.

(i) *What Mary saw* (1–2). Mark how much is said in these few words relative to TIME, PLACE, FACT, EFFECT, and TESTIMONY. It is all so spontaneous and passionate: grief and hope strangely mingle. The first evidence of the great event was given to the one who loved well enough to be at the tomb before sunrise. Early morning, and late night, hold secrets for those who embrace them.

(ii) *What Peter and John saw* (3–10). When the woman reported, the men ran, and Love (John) outran Zeal (Peter, 4). Behold these two men covering the ground early that Sabbath morning, stimulated by a nip in the air, with a light in their eyes, and a wonder in their hearts. I said that Love outran Zeal, but it was Zeal that first went into the tomb (6, 8). However, the race continues, and it is Love that first *believes* (8). Now we come to the revelations.

1. THE REVELATION TO PERSONAL DEVOTION (11–18). "*I love them that love me; and those that seek me early shall find me*" (Prov. viii. 17). The details of this section are John's only. There are

many things here which call for consideration; Mary's love and sorrow (11–15); Jesus' self-revelation and Mary's rapture (16); the two-fold command (17), and its fulfilment (18). "RABBONI *my dear Master.*" Have you ever looked up into His face and said that? How do you explain verses 17, 27, taken together? Did Jesus meanwhile ascend into heaven?

Thought : LOVE ALWAYS WINS.

ST. JOHN xx. 19-31

Title : THE NURTURE OF FAITH

19 Then the same day at evening, being the first day of the week, when the doors were shut where the disciples were assembled for fear of the Jews, came Jesus and stood in the midst, and saith unto them, Peace be unto you. 20 And when he had so said, he shewed unto them his hands and his side. Then were the disciples glad, when they saw the Lord. 21 Then said Jesus to them again, Peace be unto you : as my Father hath sent me, even so send I you. 22 And when he had said this, he breathed on them, and saith unto them, Receive ye the Holy Ghost : 23 Whose soever sins ye remit, they are remitted unto them; and whose soever sins ye retain, they are retained.

24 But Thomas, one of the twelve, called Didymus, was not with them when Jesus came. 25 The other disciples therefore said unto him, We have seen the Lord. But he said unto them, Except I shall see in his hands the print of the nails, and put my finger into the print of the nails, and thrust my hand into his side, I will not believe.

26 And after eight days again his disciples were within, and Thomas with them : then came Jesus, the doors being shut, and stood in the midst, and said, Peace be unto you. 27 Then saith he to Thomas, Reach hither thy finger, and behold my hands ; and reach hither thy hand, and thrust it into my side : and be not faithless, but believing.

28 And Thomas answered and said unto him, My Lord and my God.

29 Jesus saith unto him, Thomas, because thou

hast seen me, thou hast believed : blessed are they that have not seen, and yet have believed.

30 And many other signs truly did Jesus in the presence of his disciples, which are not written in this book : 31 But these are written, that ye might believe that Jesus is the Christ, the Son of God ; and that believing ye might have life through his name.

EXPOSITION

Connect with the preceding portion.

2. THE REVELATION TO COMMON FEAR (19–23). The former revelation (11–18) was in the morning : this is in the evening ; the former was to one ; this is to many ; the former was in the open ; this is within shut doors. The Lord manifests Himself to every variety of need, and in all sorts of places : may He reveal Himself to you to-day.

Mark carefully, the closed doors, the disciples' fear, the absence of Thomas, the new mission, and the mysterious promise. *" Then were the disciples glad when they saw the Lord."* His presence always changes fear to joy. What does verse 22 mean ? Was the Holy Spirit given before Pentecost ? Westcott translates, " *a gift of the Holy Ghost,*" even the power of the new life proceeding from the Person of the Risen Christ.

Verse 23 is difficult, but one thing is quite clear, namely, that this commission is given to the whole Church, and not to the Apostles only, or the Christian ministry ; and further, that it is an abiding commission.

3. THE REVELATION TO INDIVIDUAL DOUBT (24–29). It is very encouraging to observe Christ's care for and patience with individuals. It would seem that the Master paid a second special visit to the apostolic company in order to help Thomas. Why was he not with the others at the time of Christ's first visit ? (24). The Lord may reveal Himself in your Church one of these days when you are absent through indifference.

We talk about " doubting Thomas," but, remember, that is not the last thing we know about him. We have all doubted some time or another, but have we come to the point of saying "*my Lord and my God?*" If you have not, you are not like Thomas.

Verses 30-31 are the key to the whole of this "Gospel," the principal words being "*believe,*" and "*life.*"

Thought : "*WHOM HAVING NOT SEEN WE LOVE.*"

ST. JOHN xxi. 1-14

Title : *HUMAN AND SPIRITUAL ENTERPRISES*

1 After these things Jesus shewed himself again to the disciples at the sea of Tiberias ; and on this wise shewed he himself. 2 There were together Simon Peter, and Thomas called Didymus, and Nathanael of Cana in Galilee, and the sons of Zebedee, and two other of his disciples. 3 Simon Peter saith unto them, I go a fishing. They say unto him, We also go with thee. They went forth, and entered into a ship immediately ; and that night they caught nothing.

4 But when the morning was now come, Jesus stood on the shore : but the disciples knew not that it was Jesus.

5 Then Jesus saith unto them, Children, have ye any meat ?

They answered him, No.

6 And he said unto them, Cast the net on the right side of the ship, and ye shall find. They cast therefore, and now they were not able to draw it for the multitude of fishes.

7 Therefore that disciple whom Jesus loved saith unto Peter, It is the Lord. Now when Simon Peter heard that it was the Lord, he girt his fisher's coat unto him, (for he was naked,) and did cast himself into the sea. 8 And the other disciples came in a little ship ; (for they were not far from land, but as it were two hundred cubits,) dragging the net with fishes. 9 As soon then as they were come to land, they saw a fire of coals there, and fish laid thereon, and bread.

10 Jesus saith unto them, Bring of the fish which ye have now caught.

11 Simon Peter went up, and drew the net to land full of great fishes, an hundred and fifty and three: and for all there were so many, yet was not the net broken.

12 Jesus saith unto them, Come and dine. And none of the disciples durst ask him, Who art thou? knowing that it was the Lord. 13 Jesus then cometh, and taketh bread, and giveth them, and fish likewise.

14 This is now the third time that Jesus shewed himself to his disciples, after that he was risen from the dead.

EXPOSITION

Obviously this chapter is an Appendix or Epilogue, for the record proper finishes with xx. 30-31. The outline is as follows:—1. THE RISEN LORD'S GENERAL CARE OF HIS DISCIPLES (1-14); (i) *The Lesson* (1-8). (ii) *The Feast* (9-14). 2. THE RISEN LORD'S PARTICULAR CARE OF HIS DISCIPLES (15-23). (i) *Of Peter* (15-19). (ii) *Of John* (20-23). CONCLUSION (24-55).

It is a wonderful story. The disciples became impatient of the waiting time and, led by Peter, they went off to their fishing; but their first night out brought them no reward (1-3). In the morning the Lord appeared on the shore, and in obedience to instructions which He gave, the disciples had a great haul; whereupon they made for land (4-8). On arrival they found a meal prepared, to which Jesus invited them, and over which He presided (9-14).

In all this we see, 1. THE LIFE ATTRACTING. We must not assume that these disciples did wrong in going back to their fishing; they had to maintain themselves in some way; and Christ did not rebuke them for so doing. What a study are these men who were "together" (2): Peter, Thomas, Nathanael, James, John, and probably Andrew, and Philip. They were not to be together for long. Soon they would be widely scattered, proclaiming the Evangel, and suffering for it. Let us make the most of one another while we are "together." While we are waiting for Christ to return let us be working.

The word "*caught*" (*piazo*) is not found in the Synoptics, but eight times in this Gospel, and once in Revelation. "*Nothing*." That is a sad word here, yet, what success came of the failure (cf. chap. v). Some successes are failures, as many an one knows. Of course these men did their best, but Jesus had in store for them something better than their best. It always is so.

Jesus knew they had "caught nothing," yet, He asks them, for He would have them own to failure to prepare them for success (5). The Carpenter then tells the fishermen what to do (6). Now, Love and Zeal, John and Peter, are in the race again (7, cf. xx. 3–8, and Exposition). These men now know that this mysterious person is the Lord (12). Imagine their emotions!

Now they are His guests, and He, their Host, serves them (12, 13). What an amazing scene!

Verse 14, refers to the appearances "to the disciples" only, on Easter-day, on the following Sunday, and now.

Thought: *CHRIST CAN DO WHAT HE WILL, WHEN WE WILL DO WHAT WE CAN.*

ST. JOHN xxi. 15-25

Title: *LOVED TO THE END.*

15 So when they had dined, Jesus saith to Simon Peter, Simon, son of Jonas, lovest thou me more than these?

He saith unto him, Yea, Lord; thou knowest that I love thee.

He saith unto him, Feed my lambs.

16 He saith to him again the second time, Simon, son of Jonas, lovest thou me?

He saith unto him, Yea, Lord; thou knowest that I love thee.

He saith unto him, Feed my sheep.

17 He saith unto him the third time, Simon, son of Jonas, lovest thou me?

Peter was grieved because he said unto him the third time, Lovest thou me? And he said unto him, Lord, thou knowest all things; thou knowest that I love thee.

Jesus saith unto him, Feed my sheep.

18 Verily, verily, I say unto thee, When thou wast young, thou girdest thyself, and walkedst whither thou wouldest: but when thou shalt be old, thou shalt stretch forth thy hands, and another shall gird thee, and carry thee whither thou wouldest not. 19 This spake he, signifying by what death he should glorify God. And when he had spoken this, he saith unto him, Follow me.

20 Then Peter, turning about, seeth the disciple whom Jesus loved following; which also leaned on his breast at supper, and said, Lord, which is he that betrayeth thee? 21 Peter seeing him saith to Jesus, Lord, and what shall this man do?

22 Jesus saith unto him, If I will that he tarry till I come, what is that to thee? follow thou me.

23 Then went this saying abroad among the brethren, that that disciple should not die: yet Jesus said not unto him, He shall not die; but, If I will that he tarry till I come, what is that to thee?

24 This is the disciple which testifieth of these things, and wrote these things; and we know that his testimony is true. 25 And there are also many other things which Jesus did, the which, if they should be written every one, I suppose that even the world itself could not contain the books that should be written. Amen.

EXPOSITION

This EPILOGUE completes this Record, and returns to the PROLOGUE. At the end, as at the beginning we are in the presence of CHRIST, the LIGHT, the LOVE, and the LIFE; the *Life Attracting* (1–14), the *Love Appealing* (15–17), and the *Light Assuring* (18–25). In this portion the two latter are set forth.

2. THE LOVE APPEALING (15–17). Neither of our Versions brings out the force of this conversation

of Jesus with Peter, but Weymouth makes it plain. JESUS, "*Do you love Me?*" PETER, "*You are dear to me.*" JESUS, "*Do you love Me?*" PETER, "*You are dear to me.*" JESUS, "*Am I dear to you?*" PETER, "*You are dear to me.*" The play is upon two words translated *love*, *agapao*, and *phileo*. The former speaks of *love as principle*, and the latter, of *love as feeling*. The former is used of God's love to us, the latter of our love to one another. The former is *Divine love*, the latter is *natural love*. Now you see that Peter, who had thrice denied his Lord, is not sure of himself, and so uses the weaker word. Twice Jesus appeals to him by the stronger word, but the third time He uses Peter's word, and it was that which *grieved* the Apostle. But in his Epistles he uses Christ's first word, the word of 1 Cor. xiii. He has been gloriously restored. Will you answer Christ's question to-day?

3. THE LIGHT ASSURING (18–25). Here the veil is lifted for a moment from the future, and a glimpse is given of the end, first of Peter (18, 19), and then, of John (20–23). The former will die *unnaturally*, and the latter *naturally*. When John wrote these words the crucifixion of Peter must have been well known in the Churches. John himself died peacefully, near the close of the first century A.D. The Lord knows by what kind of death we can best glorify Him. Happy is he who dies as John died, and honoured is he who dies as Peter died. Perhaps we shall not die at all! Perhaps the Lord, instead of calling us to Him, will come for us. "*Come, Lord Jesus, come quickly.*" But whatever happens, let us follow faithfully (19, 20, 22).

Thought : OUR TIMES ARE IN HIS HANDS.

Notes

Notes

Notes

Notes

Notes

NOTES

NOTES

Notes